A MEMOIR

TYRUS

Post Hill
PRESS

A POST HILL PRESS BOOK

Just Tyrus:
A Memoir
© 2022 by Tyrus
All Rights Reserved

ISBN: 978-1-63758-066-0
ISBN (eBook): 978-1-63758-067-7

Cover design by Tiffani Shea
Cover and additional photography by Steve Randon

Post Hill Press
New York • Nashville
posthillpress.com

Published in the United States of America
1 2 3 4 5 6 7 8 9 10

This book is dedicated to all the lost boys.

Contents

Introduction

Me

You May Call Me Tyrus. My name is George T. Murdoch, but I am known as Tyrus. Before we begin, let's address the elephant in the room: *I* am the elephant in the room, standing at six feet, eight inches tall, and weighing in at 370 pounds. I also have notable tattoos that make me stand out even more. My tattoos are a combination of my visions of art and what I think would be cool. Within them are representations of my love for animals and all things nature. Now, my favorite animals are tough, but to specifically name a few, I like killer whales, leopard seals, and a good, large dog. I've incorporated some of these into my tattoos: I have a killer whale on my chest. I also have a stingray on my right hand and several others. But it's not just animals and nature I love; at the same time, I love movies, and my favorite actor is James Earl Jones. He played the bad guy, Thulsa Doom, in my favorite movie, *Conan the Barbarian*. That's why I have two interlocking snakes facing each other on my hand, symbolizing the religious cult he led. Not only do my tattoos represent things that are important to me, they also simultaneously act as a bit of a shield from people. I like that.

Just like my tattoos, my physical dimensions never go unnoticed. I am an individual with extraordinary DNA consisting of African-American and Scottish. When it comes down to it, I'm Black...but we will talk about that later.

I was a zoology major in college, but football took up too much of my time, so I switched to education and theatre. Despite my change in major and priorities, I never lost the lust for both education about and documentation of the animals we share this planet with. I love to watch them; I am still fascinated by them. I am inspired by natural historian David Attenborough...I mean *Sir* David, my real-life hero. I've watched and followed his work my whole life. This is a real passionate hobby of mine. I also support the dolphin project. Now, I hate liberals with an agenda who think they can just lay a claim on the same environment and nature that I love, that *many* love. I just don't think they have the right to act like they "own" the issue.

I've held many titles and branded many names, such as Lil Lou, Doc, George T. Clements, Migulla, Big Yella, Big Sexy Grills G, Brodus Clay, and Tyrus. In my life I have been a professional athlete, professional wrestler, entertainer, actor, a bastard child, a homeless teen, a lost cause, a thug, poor, "hood rich," a teacher, a kitchen manager, a father, a stand-up comedian, an angry kid, and a Fox News contributor. Jack of all trades, master of some. I am a professional lifetime survivor and an alpha male. For the purposes of this book and this journey, you may call me Tyrus. 'Nuff said.

Myself

I, myself, am an individual formed of many parts of many things making me who I am. While some parts are moveable, others are fixed. Who I am—my attitude, mindset, and practice—is a product of my experiences; those are immovable parts. While other people and I may go through the same experiences, they will absorb what relates to them while I absorb what relates to me. I am making the choice to write this book and offer a view inside me, but no one is allowed all of me. I had the choice to cherry-pick what is seen behind the curtain in the following pages...just like selecting specific desserts from a life-experience buffet. You choose what satisfies the desire in that moment. Sweet, filling, savory, nutritious—I chose to include what I think will provide the most satisfying parts of my story.

My existence is an unfinished book consisting of constantly changing chapter titles. My life started out with the beginnings of a children's story: it was *The Boxcar Children* turning into *A Raisin in the Sun* peppered with shades of *Sophie's Choice*, but conditions change. My life is many things mutating into a series of short stories and anecdotes that flow together, tied by common themes and interspersed with some blank pages yet to be filled.

It is no secret that I am different physically, aesthetically, verbally, as well as in both character and mindset. The difference is made obvious by my size and stature, but if that goes unnoticed, my matching attitude makes this clear. Throughout my travels around the world, I've absorbed experiences. The encounters I've had with many types of people never fail to remind me how much my own self is a creation constructed by life experiences.

Within these pages, people can and will choose what experiences or parts of *me* fit *them*. Think of this as a sarcastic self-help book, written with the intent to encourage common understanding of common sense, with the ultimate goal being to discover common ground in these uncommon political times we live in.

And I

You only get what I allow you to see...and that's my choice. Myself is for me and I control who sees in and what parts they get to view through the looking glass. I share my special moments, happy thoughts, hobbies, relationships, dark secrets, and mistakes only with whom I chose. I lack respect at times for people who share too much—which I believe is usually for attention without any intention of changing a thing. Those people seek only pity and rewarding "aww, that's so brave" responses to fill a need for some kind of validation. I've been in the room with these people. I am the guy in the room sitting back, saying to myself, "...this fucking guy...."

I will explain how the times have changed in this era of politically correct culture—with an ever-evolving narrative and standard—from what they used to be. When the common thought was "Funny thing about killing a man, you take away all he has and all he's ever going to be." It has now mutated to "Funny thing about an accusation, you take away all he has and all he's ever going to be." We will also attempt to look at how political events directly affect us or how life goes on in spite of those events. Reading this book will encourage one to not take things so seriously in this crazy world and, at the same time, take issues on a case-by-case basis. Maybe changing the view from tribalism to do-what's-best-for-me-ism. It's okay to disagree with your tribe; tribes are not sports teams. This book will give readers insight into how my brain works and my thought processes—where common sense and life experience come into play and not what side of the fence I live on.

Why Now?

For a lot of years, people have watched me out in the public—in the ring—basically as a performer. That's fine. But what I do now is a little bit different. Being on television and using my words as a career comes with a whole different set of rules. And don't people want to understand where I'm coming from? For me, television isn't that different than wrestling. Before the lights come on and it's time to start the show, I'm stressed out. Nervous. Already second-guessing myself. But once it's go time? That's when I step up. That's when I do what I do. Preparation, discipline, having a plan but still being spontaneous are how I approach my business. I was like that as a football player. As a bodyguard. As a wrestler. And now as a political and social commentator. Anyway, now that people are hearing my voice every day and listening to my words, I want them to know what I'm really about. I want you, the reader, to understand where I'm coming from. The stakes are different for me now. I feel like I have a lot to say and a lot to share. I'm going to do that in this book. Maybe it's an exercise, the chance for me to figure out a little bit more about who I am. That's okay, too. Bottom line: once you finish reading this book, you'll know a lot more about me. And if I can get you thinking about certain things, who knows? Maybe you'll learn a lot more about yourself, too. Never too late to learn about yourself, right? Okay, let's get to it.

CHAPTER 1

In the Beginning

J did not have an easy beginning. My home was broken before I entered it. I'll explain more in little bit, but when I made my first appearance in this place in February 1973, had I known what lay ahead in the immediate future, I probably would've turned right back around in my mother's womb before yelling to the doctor, "Leave me the hell alone! I am not coming out!"

My dad's family had a farm. My grandfather, his dad, had made a lot of money in stocks, but he eventually was wiped out by the demands from his fourteen-plus kids, my father included. I did like going to that farm. I could always tell my mother was uncomfortable there, however, because despite how terrible my father treated her, his mother did nothing but praise him and talk endlessly about what a wonderful son he was. Whether she was ignorant or just plain clueless or maybe a little of both, I don't know. But for her to not realize what her son was, I'm sorry—I mean, I could tell at four years old the damage he was doing to my mother.

Living with my parents, it was just chaos all the time. When I was about three years old, my parents left me in the car while they went into a store. I waited and waited and waited. It started to feel like they had forgotten about me, so I climbed into the driver's seat of the yellow Datsun we had (the proper term for the model, I believe, was "piece of shit"), and I started the thing up. The keys had been left in the ignition. I figured if they were not coming to get me then I would just drive myself home. I threw it into reverse, backed up, and hit the car behind me. Of course, that's when they came running out. Thankfully, my mother was able to talk her way out of any responsibility with the other driver. Was that my fault? Of course not. I was just three years old. I was simply reacting to the disorganization and dysfunction that surrounded me 24/7.

My father would go on these five- or six-day benders and I knew whenever he got home, things were going to be ugly. His biggest fear—I mean, his absolute obsession—with my mom was her cheating on him. The irony to that is all he did was cheat on her. Even at four years old, I knew how fucked up the situation was. My mom was like a 1970s waif, almost like a hippie; a good wind would've taken her away. She was barely twenty years old, putting up with his bullshit every moment of her life. We had this pepper plant on the windowsill and I would crack her up when I would break off one of those little red chilies and chew it up. It was hellfire in my mouth, but it made my mom laugh and that's all I cared about. Putting some light in her day. That's what it was all about. That laughter of hers when I would chew those peppers up brought at least a little bit of light to an otherwise bleak existence. We were living in a little two-bedroom apartment up on the thirty-second floor of a tenement in Lynn, Massachusetts. Cheap green shag carpeting and peeling linoleum tile in the kitchen and bathroom. It was a cramped, angry little world where every moment hinged on when he might come bursting through that door to wreak some more havoc. Something else you have to understand: in the 1970s, living in the Boston area, my parents were basically fugitives. That's because there was a law against interracial couples that was not rescinded until 1986! Seriously. Look it up. I'm not making excuses for them, but imagine having that pressure over your head—that you were basically fugitives on the run simply for being married.

Something else that always struck me weird about my father was that he cried a lot. He was very emotional. That confused me because of how violent he could be. It didn't make sense that he was, at least to me, emotionally complicated. But it's just how he was. He was the last of fourteen brothers and sisters so I'm sure his upbringing wasn't that easy. He was a pretty big guy—six foot two—and they called him "Red" because his hair had a reddish tint to it. His skin was a deep mahogany color and he was a tough dude. My mom was just about five foot five and weighed maybe 130 pounds. Barely. So no real match there when he came busting in. Once he got home, it was basically for sex and food and then off on the road again; he worked on moving trucks. Once he came home to start trouble, I would usually head under the bed. That was my spot. I could see what was going on, but he couldn't see me. My little home away from home. Shelter from the storm.

My mom would be so afraid when the front door opened and I knew it. I felt it. I could see it in her eyes, one last glimpse of panic and confusion before I darted to my usual spot.

All I wanted to do was help her, but I had no real idea what to do. Down there under the bed with my face buried in that ugly green shag carpet, I could sometimes hear other battered wives dealing with their own monsters in nearby apartments. Shattered cries breaking across the dank courtyards morning, noon, and night. It's like they were all in the same boat. One big fucking horror show. But my attention was focused on my own particular nightmare.

My brother was only two years old at this time and he remained pretty much in the background. It was a good strategy: don't cry a lot, stay quiet, avoid attracting attention to yourself. But I mean, at two years old, he was also unaware of much of what was going on. I know it sounds weird that I knew so much at four years old, but honestly, I've always felt like back then, I was a man in a kid's body. I just never felt like much of a kid.

I don't have very vivid memories of my brother back then. But I do know that we had a couple of cats in the apartment and those kept us entertained. We would sit there draping blankets around them, pretending they were superheroes. Subconsciously, I was probably figuring out a way to try and fly out of the place where I was trapped.

My mom used to braid my dad's hair. That was one of the things he used her for because she was really good at it. But her hands would tremble when she did it because if she got one braid wrong, if something was not to his liking, he would go off on her. This one night, he came back home and I was peeking out and I knew things were worse than usual. He was raging. She did something to his hair he didn't like, and he hit her, harder than usual. I was four years old. And something snapped. Enough was enough. I crawled out from under the bed, quickly went into the kitchen, and grabbed a good-sized knife. Not a butter knife. A steak knife. A business knife. He didn't see me coming until the last split second when I rushed him, cocked my arm back, and prepared to drive that shiny blade into whatever part of his body I hit. I wasn't aiming specifically; I just wanted this motherfucker to stop hitting my mother and it felt like a switch had flipped in my brain.

He turned just in time to see my arm coming down and he caught it before the knife hit him. My father looked at me like, "What the fuck do you think you are doing?" In one angry move, he grabbed the knife out of my hand and threw me over his shoulder and headed for the window of the apartment. *This will all be over pretty quickly*, I thought to myself. My mother blocked his way and calmly talked some sense into him. "He was protecting his mother! Put him down!" My father, even in his rage, had to know tossing his kid out of a thirty-second-story window was not the move to make. He dropped me and walked out. My mind was racing.

Most kids at this age are having books read to them, they're playing with friends, they are being nurtured. I was pulling a knife on my father because he was beating my mother—again. I think I went into a little bit of shock. I figured out later what was going through his mind when he carried me toward the window. He had decided at that moment that I was not his son. It was like all of his paranoia and suspicions came true right before his eyes. After all, no son of his would ever pull a knife on him; at least, that was how he saw it. Always the victim. Evidently, he was also convinced that my brother wasn't his either, not that he ever pulled a knife on him, but because he was weak and small. My father was very self-important and wanted to believe things about himself that just were not true.

The next night I was back under my bed waiting for God knows what to happen when I heard the door open. I heard strange voices. Right in front of my wide eyes, I saw a pair of work boots. It was my grandfather. My mom's dad. Evidently, he was there to take my mom, my brother, and me away. So began the next chapter of my life. We packed up right then and there and later that night I got to experience some more drama.

My grandparents had a house nearby that was close to a lake. Open space. Normal, I guess you could say. I had never seen their home and I automatically fell in love with it. I had never met my maternal grandparents in person before, so this was like being abducted by aliens. They took us to their house and we went from living in what felt like a closet to occupying a two-story mini mansion.

When I finally met my maternal grandmother, I understood why they called her "the General." Regal and powerful, she sat there at the table like a boss. I was very comfortable with it. I liked her energy. She projected power, and I found that cool. She also made grilled cheese sandwiches the likes of which are still unequaled in my mind. Along with a bowl of her homemade tomato soup, these were created, artisan, gourmet grilled cheese sandwiches. It made me realize there was a whole other world out there, away from the government cheese I was used to. Yes, I liked how she rolled. I can't imagine what was going on in her mind. Meeting her Black grandsons for the very first time. She seemed to take it all in stride, which made me comfortable. We were there probably a month or so. There were lots of meetings in the kitchen that I could tell were important. Everybody speaking in hushed, serious tones. Even though I couldn't make out exactly what was getting said, I knew it was a big deal. My grandfather, I could tell, was not going to let my brother and me live there. He wasn't an emotional guy; I just don't think he wanted the taboo attached to bringing in two Black kids to a white neighborhood where everybody knew each other. A very tight-knit place. It was confusing for everybody in the family. My mom had not seen her parents in years. There were lots of adjustments that needed to take place and it was a very unnatural situation for everyone. The family didn't need the scandal.

My brother and I could've ended up in a lot of places, separated. My grandfather, as strongly as he felt we could not live with him, was still adamant that we stay together. I give him a lot of credit for that. That's why we ended up staying in the home where we wound up, in the town of nearby Peabody with John and Ann, who basically fostered us while also helping take care of other kids in a daycare capacity—mostly military kids whose parents had been given deployments. I heard later that some money had to change hands to make that happen and I'll always be thankful to my grandfather for doing that. I originally wished we could've stayed with him, but at least he wasn't giving us up for dead. At least he cared about keeping me and my little brother together.

After I moved in with John and Ann, I heard that my father showed up once at my grandparents' house, demanding to know where I was. My mom's father met him with a rifle and told him to basically get the fuck out. So that took care of that. When my mom visited us at the house in Peabody, it was more like a friend coming to see us than a parent. I think she knew she had been replaced by people who really knew what they were doing and genuinely cared about our well-being. She would hang out, watching television or something, but there wasn't any sort of real closeness.

John was a funny guy. He was a "Coke man" in that he worked for Coca-Cola most of his life. I think straight out of the military that's what he went to work as—a truck driver for Coke. And those Coke guys were real company men. In fact, one day, Ann took a taste test at a local mall and actually picked Pepsi over Coke. John's reaction to this was worse than had she had an affair behind his back. She tried explaining that the Coke was warm and the Pepsi had been served on ice, but no dice. John was not having it. To him, even warm Coke was better than the iciest Pepsi. Company guy through and through.

CHAPTER 2

Fighting = Friendship (Manhood Starts at Seven)

I learned early that the first thing kids did when you went to a new school—that is, if you looked different than they did—was to pick on you. Trust me, I didn't take any of that shit. I was good with my fists. Even in kindergarten, I knew how to fight. Some wise guy might think he was getting the best of me by getting me into a headlock, but he had no clue. When I started punching, hard left, some hard rights, word got around pretty quickly that messing with me was not a good idea. I mean, I was taking on third graders. I couldn't figure out why they would make fun of the color of my skin, but it didn't really matter to me.

If they wanted to pick a fight, I was in it to win it—and I usually did. That said, once they were down, I would help them up. I could see that they learned their lesson and oftentimes, we became friends. That happened with this kid named Jerry. We got into a little scrap on the school bus one day: nothing too serious, but we became friends afterward. He was a Jewish kid who kids also picked on because of his frizzy hair. They called it a "Jew fro" as they mocked him. Well, nobody makes fun of my friends. So one day I got into it with this big third-grader on behalf of Jerry. I was doing okay, but then this kid, who was a lot bigger, started getting the best of me. I was in trouble. Jerry picked up his book bag, which was loaded with some seriously big, hardback textbooks, and he let swing. By accident, he hit me right in the face and knocked me down. The bigger kid actually stopped and said to me, "Hey kid, are you okay?" Thanks, Jerry!

One thing about Ann: she really dressed me to the nines for school. I was pimped out. Clip-on ties, all kinds of fancy duds—but there was nothing better than the maroon corduroy day suit. Damn. That thing was crazy. Matching jacket and pants and just as smooth as could be. When I put it on to go to school that day, Ann was clear. "We need to keep these clothes clean. They're very nice and they cost a lot of money. You need to take care of them." Looking back, I really believe that she dressed me up nice like this because she thought it would help me stop fighting. If I knew that I would get punished for messing up my clothes, then maybe I wouldn't get into so many scraps. She was smart. She raised us with a combination of love and consistency. We knew the rules. I knew I would get spanked if I got those clothes dirty.

So I went to school that day and of course wound up on the jungle gym. Today there are no more jungle gyms, right? Back then kids were allowed to have serious fun. Seesaws, jungle gyms, those merry-go-round things that you push in a circle... Why can't kids play on those anymore? Don't get me started. That's for another book. Anyway, I started on the jungle gym and then went out to the playing field. I was climbing, messing around, just having a good old day. I kind of forgot about the clothes until I got on the school bus going home. My brother pointed out a grass-stained tear on one of the knees. "Fuck," I said; I cussed like an adult, even at seven years old. Jaws always dropped when I cussed, especially on the bus, because nobody did that at seven years old. I knew there was a problem, though. My brother along with a few other kids started singing this sweet harmony like Boyz II Men, "You're in trouble...you're gonna get it..." I didn't want to hear it. I didn't need songs at that point. I needed a plan and I quickly concocted one.

When I got home, I went into my room, got out of the clothes, and buried the suit at the bottom of the hamper before putting on my play clothes. Mission accomplished, right? Wrong. You see, every day when I got home, Ann would normally have to tell me to get in my play clothes, and then I would leave my school clothes thrown all over the house. So it looked very weird when she saw me come out in my play clothes without being asked, and also when there was nothing thrown around the room. You have to remember, her nickname for me was her "Little Tornado." So she went looking in the bedroom and then in the hamper and she figured out what had happened. I had made it worse by using my pencil eraser to try and get the stains off my knees and she noticed that as well. I had pretty much ruined this expensive and beautiful maroon corduroy day suit. I was outside playing when she called. Inside, some of the kids attending daycare there, along with my brother, were already in timeout for too much horsing around. Ann was not happy.

"I told you to keep your clothes clean. I told you over and over. And now you have to get punished and I know that you know that." With that, she pulled out the metal spatula. This thing didn't just sting when it hit your ass; it cast a glint of light off the metal, kind of like a *Star Wars* lightsaber—but with very bad intentions. Something snapped inside me. This was the first time she ever saw my "dad" emerging in my personality. I picked up a nearby barstool. She kind of smirked at me and said, "Are you going to hit me?"

"Yeah," I said.

"You do it and that it will be a big mistake." She barely got out the last part of that sentence before I swung away, hitting her so hard the barstool shattered all over the room. I learned later that I not only cracked her orbital socket but also busted her collarbone badly. I still can't believe this happened and that I'm writing these words. Of all the bad things I've done in my life, this may be the worst. It haunted me then. It haunts me now. It will always haunt me. But it did, it happened, and I knew I had to get out of there.

CHAPTER 3

Running Away

I had to run away. I quickly packed up some snacks, basically some Capri Sun juice packs and some Devil Dog cakes, and then I was out of there. The front door was locked so I had to exit through the garage. John was in there hanging out, oblivious to anything that had happened. I couldn't get the door open and he said, "Let me help you there," and so then I was free. My initial plan in my head was to get back to my grandparents' house. Now, I had no idea where my grandparents lived. My plan was to just head over the ridge and hope for the best. In reality, they were miles away. But I was only seven years old, so what the hell did I know?

A neighbor saw me and questioned me about where I was going. He clearly was concerned so he tricked me and got me to go to his backyard, saying he would help me. Once I knew he had gotten the best of me, I did all I could do to at least get some space between me and him. I climbed a tall tree in the yard. All hell broke loose after that. The fire department showed up and after several minutes those guys started getting very pissed that I was wasting their day when there was real work to be done around the area. They called my mother and she came over. I wasn't budging for her either. Finally, John came over. He said to me, "Get out of that tree right now." That was it. John, I would listen to. I climbed down and he and I started walking home. Everybody was screaming around us, but not John. He was as calm as could be. As we reached the house, Ann was being wheeled out on a stretcher. She turned to us and said, "Please don't hurt my baby." That's how decent she was. No matter what I had done, she still cared about me. She cut me some slack. She knew the environment I came out of. Man, just thinking about that right now gives me goose bumps. That's what she was thinking as they took her to the hospital.

Once we got in the house, I was still very agitated. I was pissed off. I was frustrated. I didn't like what my life was at that moment. "I want to go live with my dad," I said to John.

"Go ahead and call him," John said. He got me the phone—he even dialed the number and then handed me the receiver.

"Dad, come take me away from here. I want to come live with you."

There wasn't even a pause. "No. We can't be together. You need to live your life and I need to live mine."

And with that, I heard the click. So much for that plan. John, who was standing there and, I think, was smart enough to figure out what happened, said to me firmly, "Go to your room and calm down." So I did. I lay on my bed and my mind started to slow down. I started coming back down to earth. A couple of hours later there was a knock on my door and it was John. He told me to follow him downstairs and so I did. When we got to the living room, he set me down on the couch, looked me in the eye firmly, and said, "Listen to me, young man. You hit my wife and you caused great harm. Nobody is going to do that and not get punished, do you understand me?" I nodded silently. In that moment, I knew exactly what he was talking about. I had earned the punishment I knew I was about to receive.

It wasn't like when I had been living with my father and he would arbitrarily smack me upside the head. I could never make sense of his violence toward my mother or me or anybody else. A backhand slap out of the blue, for nothing. Okay, I'm sure some drugs and alcohol affected his behavior, but that's no excuse for striking a child like that. With John, it made sense. I knew I had done something terrible and there was a price to be paid for that. He took out a belt. A thick, leather belt. Maybe he gave me ten spanks with it. It was something like that. And I deserved every one of them and more. It hurt me, but with each one, I understood more and more that what I had done was terrible and that I could not do it again. I mean, I knew I was going to keep getting in fights at school and in life. But striking a woman like that? Someone who was so kind to me, someone who cared about nurturing me? Never again.

I went back upstairs after he was done with me and a short while later there was another knock on the door. It was John, with a couple of bowls of ice cream. That was really the day John and Ann became Mom and Dad to me. I still feel terrible for what I did to her; I genuinely do. I will always regret that day. And I was so happy when she fully recovered. But the lessons I learned that day I continue to live by today and I have passed them on to my children. Trust, respect, dignity, decency, and responsibility are standards that I hold very high because of what happened that day. After that incident,

John and I became even more inseparable. He cut people's hair on the weekends; he was such a hard worker. I would go watch him. I learned about hard work from him. There would be countless other days that he would spend with me looking for frogs in the front yard, even when he probably knew there were none. He took me under his wing. He loved me unconditionally and he became my father.

About a year later my world got rocked again. I came home from school one day and something had changed in the house. Something was very different. The entire atmosphere had shifted. John was sitting in his chair, drinking a glass of sherry. He looked like he had been crying. I had never seen him shed a tear. He was a tough guy who didn't show a lot of emotion. Something bad had obviously happened. When his daughter walked to the room, she was crying too, and in the kitchen, I could see Ann hiding her tears. Man, the whole house was crying.

"Sit down," he said to me gently. "We have to talk to you about something." And then he explained to me that they had heard from my mom. She had graduated from nursing school and was moving to California. John and Ann had been in the process of trying to legally adopt my brother and me. My mother decided she wanted us back and wanted to take us to California with her. The way the legal system was then, there was nothing they could do to keep us. Later on, my mother would tell my brother and me that they had not fought for us and so they probably didn't really love us. But that was total bullshit. She was just trying to erase her past and move ahead with us after they had done all of the heavy lifting. They had raised us. Even as a kid, I smelled a rat. I knew John and Ann loved us like we were their own. But there was nothing we could do. I had no idea what it was going to be like, leaving the house that had become such a safe and secure environment. I was scared shitless.

CHAPTER 4

Putting a Good Spin on Things

Everything was just so awkward. Ann was about to try and put a good spin on things, but I could tell something was really wrong. She said, looking at me, "We have some really good news. We heard from your mom; she really misses you and she's moved to California. She wants you to be part of her life again and so she is going to fly you out there to be with her."

I was a little kid; I didn't have any concept of what Massachusetts was or what California was or how far away these places were or anything like that. I only had one thought on my mind. One single concern. "When can I come back? How soon can I come home and sleep in my bed?"

They both looked at each other and I knew there was no good answer. That's one thing I learned early in life; I knew when I was being lied to because it happened so frequently. I was a connoisseur of dishonesty. I could see it coming a mile away, or when it was just two inches in front of my face, like right now. I give them credit, though. They were trying to put a smile on, but I could see deep into their eyes that they knew that I knew what was going on. But what were they doing?

They were being good parents. They were trying to protect us and create a buffer for the pain. They genuinely wanted us to believe this was a good foot forward. They wanted to guide us through this clearly uncomfortable situation and create as positive a spin as they could. They talked about getting on a plane, how fun and exciting that would be, and how beautiful California was. For me, it had the opposite effect. It scared me because all of a sudden it was all about a sense of the unknown. My friends, my room, my stuff—what was going to happen to that world? Who was going to help John at the barbershop? I didn't want my little world dismantled. It worked for me. It was healthy and comfortable. But unfortunately, the choice was made for me.

Two days later, my brother and I were off to California. My mother didn't fly back, choosing instead to send one of her friends for us. I was so torn. At this time in my life, my mom had become like a buddy to me. She was a friend whenever she came to visit. But she wasn't my "mom." With Ann and John, we had vacations and structure and rules. We had a family life. I still had a lot of trust issues with my mom and I wasn't quite sure how it was all going to go down.

My brother and I were met at the airport by yet another friend of hers and taken way out to a place called Sunland-Tujunga, which is part of the San Fernando Valley. Very white, not many Brothers. When we got to the house, which seemed pleasant enough from the outside, we didn't see my mom, who supposedly was at work. Her friend showed us to our bedroom, which had the same green shag carpeting that was found throughout most of the house. The room was pretty much bare bones. There was a single mattress on the floor, and that's where my brother and I crashed. Some hours later,

I opened my eyes and was very disoriented. You know those moments when you wake up and you don't quite know where you are? I saw a closet across the room with a few things hanging, but not much else. I got up, rubbed my eyes, and started padding around the place. There didn't seem to be anybody else there, but I found out later my mom's roommate, an attractive young girl like my mom, was sleeping. I wandered outside and discovered a small, unkempt, sunburnt backyard. No care whatsoever. Weeds and dead shrubs, punished by too many hundred-degree days. I saw a grapefruit tree, something that was new to me. Beneath the tree was a ton of spoiled fruit on the ground. Nobody was tending to anything here. That smell of rotting citrus got picked up by the dry, parching wind and was carried throughout the entire property. I stepped around the rotting yellow rinds and went back inside into the kitchen where I found a phone mounted on wall.

As I dialed John and Ann's number, I noticed a big cockroach wandering around the sink. They never would've allowed living conditions like this. This place was depressing. Their home was happy, clean, and spotless. I was already yearning for those Sunday mornings when I would wake up, smell bacon frying and just know that John had returned from the donut shop. I would make my way to the kitchen and pick one of my favorites, one that was leaking sweet purple grape jelly. That was John's favorite and so that was mine too. Now that world really seemed to be gone as I watched the cockroach try to scramble up the side of the sink.

"George!" Ann exclaimed as she heard my voice. I think she forgot this was all supposed to be a good idea. She quickly remembered she couldn't act like she missed me too much. The first thing I told her was that I wanted to come and visit them. She said to me that they missed me very much and that when the time was right, we would be able to see each other. But I started getting that feeling again that I wasn't being told the truth. Ann tried hard, telling me my mother did the responsible thing by making sure we were taken care of because her parents wouldn't allow us to live in their home. Being separated from her kids was hard on my mom, and we needed to respect what she was doing because she was doing her best. Some of that still makes sense to me today. I really can't criticize my mom that much because I think she did make the best decisions she could, given the circumstances. Her goal at that point was to pick up where we had left off. I didn't think what had been done was malicious. She had begun working as a registered nurse—working very hard—and I really believe she was doing her best. But back then, as a little kid, it was hard to get over the fact that I felt abandoned by her.

I said goodbye, hung up the phone, and slept a bit more until my mom came home from work. It was definitely uncomfortable for the first couple of days. We were all on edge. But after about five days when I went to call John and Ann again, my mom took the phone from my hand and hung it up before the connection could go through. "You're not going to call them anymore, okay? They were paid to take care of you; do you understand that? And that's over now, so you're not going to see them and you're not going to call them. This is your new life now, okay? And everything is going to be okay." And that was that.

That first week I was playing outside the house, just bouncing a ball or whatever because I didn't know anybody in the neighborhood, and this kid, James, came over to me and said, "I don't like niggers in my neighborhood." Yes, that's what he said to me. Before I go on, I should explain, as I learned later (although it should be obvious to all of you) he had no idea what that word meant. He obviously grew up in a household where it had been casually tossed around, and he was just repeating it. That's the problem with words like that. Kids mimic them—like, they mimic *everything* their parents say. Kids aren't racist.

Anyway, James was older, probably nine, and he was bigger. Now, I need to explain something here, too. Even at seven years old I could tell that fighting was different on the West Coast than it was on the East Coast. I had already learned plain as day when somebody walked up and started talking trash, game was on, automatically. Out there in California, evidently, they liked to do some talking. Then he said something that truly blew my mind. "Hey nigger, you can throw the first punch, go ahead." Well, I was more than happy to take him up on his offer. I pulled back, swung away, and laid him out on the front yard, practically knocking him out cold with one punch. And that wasn't all. I then had my knees on his chest, wailing away on him until his mother and sister came out of the house and pulled me off. I beat him and I beat him good.

But guess what? The next day we became best friends. It all went back to my fighting on the East Coast. It was how I made friends. We never fought again; it was all just a rite of passage. He knew not to mess with me anymore and he respected me. In today's culture, maybe you would unfriend him or try and cancel him. But back in the day, you didn't freak out. You respected people that didn't take your shit. I'll add that he and I are still friends today. That's what a true bond of love is. And he doesn't have an ounce of racism in him. I think our friendship was helpful in that sense. He was smart enough to think for himself and judge me for what I was, not because of what color I was, but because of what kind of kid I was.

I remember one day my mom called her roommate a "nymphomaniac." I didn't know what that word meant, of course, but judging from her behavior, it became obvious pretty quickly. She constantly had guys in and out of that house. I'd hear them. I would hear sounds like animals, lots of moaning and grunting. And the next day somebody else would be there. And the next day somebody else. These guys would be in the house, eating our food and drinking our milk and orange juice and basically taking over. I thought that was bullshit. Instinctively I knew I had to look out for my brother and myself. I knew I had to have a stash of money just in case we needed to survive, and so I devised a little plan. Oftentimes when these guys came over, they would leave their wallets on the kitchen counter or maybe on a table by the couch. I decided that for all of the wear and tear on our home, my brother and I deserved a cut. So I started taking some money. A little bit here and there from all the different guys. Fives, tens, and maybe a twenty. Eventually, I had about a thousand dollars in cash tucked away in our bedroom. One day, the roommate called me out and confronted me about what was going on. She told me this wasn't right and that I had to give the money back, but I was telling her, no, I needed that to make sure I had food for my brother and me. That it was my survival instinct kicking in. But she still took the money back and gave it back to the guys. She never told my mother, however, which I appreciated.

CHAPTER 5

An Interesting Place to Grow Up

It was a pretty bohemian scene around the house. Lots of pot being smoked, lots of drinking, and lots of free-spirited sex. You never knew what you were going to see when you opened up one of the bedroom doors. Not the healthiest environment for young kids, but it was what was. I never really felt settled, in large part because every six months or so we would move. We stayed around the same Sunland-Tujunga area, but it was hard to put down any kind of roots with all of the moves. But I was collecting my share of pets. I remember seeing a Doberman in the pet store; he was, like, 500 bucks, and I knew I could never afford that. So I started catching things. Lizards, snakes, a cat stuck up in a tree—whatever I could get my hands on, I caught it. That instinct has stuck with me and I still have a lot of interesting and unusual pets.

One place where we lived was the best because the neighborhood was full of kids like me who just loved catching things. We called ourselves "the snake hunters" and decided that we were all going to become millionaires by catching snakes all over town. It was lots of open space in the Valley back then and there were many catching opportunities. On weekends, we would all meet on our bikes after having packed up our lunches and we would head off into the wild. *Stand by Me* had nothing on us. I remember that one day I lifted up this big rock on a hot summer day, and hiding underneath was a baby rattlesnake. This was a whole different ballgame. Rat snakes, racers, king snakes, gopher snakes; those were fine—those couldn't hurt you. The rattlesnakes, though, were badass. They could do you in. While my buddies flipped out, I calmly went into my house and got a pair of my mom's salad tongs. I lifted the rock back up, grabbed the snake by the neck, and popped it into my canvas sack. Jaws dropped all around me. I was now the king of the snake hunters.

As time went on, I started finding my way. I tested very high in school and was bumped up to a magnet program, which made me feel good. Even though we were moving a lot, I was starting to look forward and, as sad as it seems, the memories of Ann and John were fading fast in the rearview mirror. Over time, I lost John and Ann's number, which really meant I could never speak to them again. If you didn't have a phone number back then, you had nothing. I didn't know what their exact address was so I couldn't even write them. Eventually, my mom started dating this guy who looked exactly like John Denver. Interestingly, his name was Ross, which automatically scored a couple of points in my book.

Ross was different than other guys my mom brought home. He seemed serious and responsible. He also did something nobody else had ever done with me: He sat me down and said, "I want to talk to you." He said he wanted to marry my mother. He looked me straight in the eyes and told me that I and my brother meant something to him and he was going to do everything he could to be a father figure to us. Nobody ever spoke to me like that. He was a good man who cared about our feelings. Whenever our birthdays rolled around, he was right there with great gifts. Took us to the movies, to ball games; he really was a wonderful guy. I got used to him being in my life. He was a plumber who came from Colorado, and he would tell us all about his dream—to build a big house back in Colorado and have us all there with him. I started playing Little League baseball and was having great luck with that and he was always right there cheering me on. It really did start to feel like family life.

One night, my mother made plans for my brother and me to go stay over at a friend's house. It was kind of unusual. Neither of us felt like going but she was adamant. It almost felt like she wanted us out of the house for some reason. My brother and I went over there and spent the night, and when I woke up in the morning, I didn't like what they were serving for breakfast. All I wanted was my Cap'n Crunch Berries cereal. So I walked back over to my house, opened the door, and boom. There was a guy in his underwear sitting at the kitchen table, chowing down on my Cap'n Crunch cereal. He was looking at me and I was looking at him and things were not good. He called out over his shoulder, "Who the fuck is this?" The bedroom door opened and out walked my mom in her bra and panties. My mom told me I needed to go back over to my friend's house immediately. She insisted, and I said to her, "I want to call Ross," and she said, "You're not going to call Ross," and she basically marched me out of the house and slammed the door. I was furious. I didn't let my little brother know what was happening because I always tried to protect him from this kind of crap. All I wanted to do was call Ross. I wanted to call him and tell him I was upset. I wanted him to come over and throw out this guy who was eating my Cap'n Crunch.

When my brother and I went back to the house, I noticed a motorcycle in the driveway. *Okay, that's the guy's bike*, I thought to myself. We went in and as it turned out, my mom's roommate had also brought one of these guys home and the four of them were lounging around the house like we didn't even belong there. I did not like this one bit. I was sitting outside the house later that day with a buddy and Ross pulled up—but he didn't seem like himself. I was so happy to see him but he looked down. He looked broken. He was pale and sweaty and I could tell something was on his mind.

"Georgie," he said to me, "I hate to tell you this, but your mother is not going to marry me. Which means I can't see you anymore. I want to see you. I love you guys. But it's just not going to be possible." He wrote down his phone number and handed it to me, saying, "You can call me if you ever need anything. I'm really going to miss you."

After Ross drove away, I crumbled up the number and threw it on the ground.

My friend said, "Why did you do that?"

I said, "Because he's not coming back. Phone numbers don't matter."

"But he's your dad," my friend said.

"He's not my dad," I answered. "I don't have a dad."

After a few weeks, this lowlife biker was still kind of living in our house, and my mom sat me down and said, "Listen, you need to understand I thought I had ovarian cancer, and when I met Ross I thought he would be a good man to take care of you and your brother. But as it turns out, I don't have cancer and I genuinely don't want to spend my life with him. I know it's hard to understand, but it just is not meant to be. I just wanted him in case I was gone." Another example of my mom trying to do the right thing by making sure my brother and I were being taken care of in her absence. But once again I just hurt like hell when the concept of potential stability got yanked away.

Then the biker guy, whose name was Craig, moved in officially. No job, no nothing. Just a lowlife shacking up with my mom and being a complete fucking prick, 24/7. He didn't like me because he knew I was onto him. He knew that I knew what he was all about—that he was just a freeloader. We had lots of confrontations. I wanted nothing to do with him, but he was always baiting me. Little confrontations became heated and we would start fighting. He would hit me, and he would hit me pretty hard. I lost every time. I would wind up on the floor crying, mad at myself because I let him get me. Some cheap shot to the stomach or something. But I'll tell you what, I sucked it up every time. I pulled myself up off the floor and I showed him I could take it. And every time I got up, I got a little bit stronger. I was "Hulking" up. That's what I was thinking about. The whole time in my head I kept saying, "One day I'm going to whip his ass. One day I'm really going to whip his ass but good."

I was watching a lot of television in those days. That's where my role models really came from. *The Incredible Hulk* was it for me. That was my show. That's who and what I wanted to be. But it wasn't just fantasizing about getting stronger, it was about doing right by people. I also loved the show *Good Times*. A Black family living in the projects in Chicago—their struggle seemed real to me. There weren't many Black kids in my school, so that became my Black experience. J.J., played by Jimmie Walker, was just brilliant. He helped me escape. I also loved watching wrestling. Wrestling played a big part in my life. Good guys versus bad guys. Lots of reluctant heroes. I liked that. That's what I aspired to be. A reluctant hero. Someone that didn't go looking for trouble but, rather, dealt with it when it arrived.

CHAPTER 6

America's Relationship with Wrestling

I've always been fascinated by America's relationship with pro wrestling. What makes it so unique? Well, for one thing, wrestling is almost always available to watch. Boxing, at least with the big names, doesn't happen all that much. The NFL is just once a week. But with wrestling, it's there almost every day if you want to look for it. It's constant. So for fans, they can always be connected to their favorite stars. Another aspect of wrestling that I think makes it a perfect fit for American audiences, especially, is the storytelling. If you think about it, a lot of it goes back to the Old West. It's black hats and white hats. There's no real mystery who the bad guys are and who the good guys are. The lines are drawn early, and they are always very sharp and clear. Americans love great stories where the good guy eventually comes out the victor. It may take a while and there are bound to be many twists and turns, but in the end, you can usually count on the good guy emerging victorious.

Compared with boxing, there's also the timing factor. Any boxing match can end in the first round and that's it. You are guaranteed nothing. Wrestling is exactly the opposite. You are always going to get a complete show. It's like Broadway in that respect. It's well thought out, the characters are tightly drawn, and emotional beats are distinct, consistent, and carefully plotted. You always get your money's worth. In fact, most times you get far more than your money's worth. I'm not saying it's 100 percent orchestrated and scripted. Not at all. There are absolutely spontaneous moments within the course of any professional wrestling performance. But at the end of the day, it is a performance.

Now, for those that want to whine and call it "fake," my answer is simple. Have you ever gone to the movies? Do you think what Arnold Schwarzenegger is doing is real? Of course not. So why do you suspend reality for movies and not professional wrestling? It's essentially the same thing. It's high-concept entertainment built around heroes and villains. The art of simulating combat is revered, especially in Japan. It's considered an art form, in fact. At its heart, that's what professional wrestling is. Not to mention the fact that you have to be in incredible shape to perform at the highest levels that professional wrestling demands. Yes, there are scenarios that are worked out beforehand, but you still need to execute them and make them look and feel good. That doesn't just happen. That comes from thousands of hours of training, every day of the year. It's extremely hard work and the margins of error are microscopic. You can get seriously injured if things aren't done just right. Wrestling stars definitely have become like movie stars. If it's someone's passion to try and ruin the magic show by constantly crying that wrestling is "fake," then I don't want to be around them. They're not the kind of person who interests me.

Of course, another reason that bolsters America's deep and passionate dedication to professional wrestling is the fact that it's carried on a number of high-profile outlets. Between the WWE and the TBS Superstation, there's always a lot of programming for fans to latch onto and live with for a while. Something for everybody, all the time. For lots of personal reasons, I'm happy that America embraces professional wrestling. But even if I had not been involved myself, it's something I've always appreciated. Say whatever you want about professional wrestling; it's successful. Damn successful. They know what they are doing and they give the audience what they want. That's an American tradition as old as vaudeville. And I don't think it will ever stop. At least not in my lifetime.

When I was about thirteen, I was wrestling with some of my friends and Craig came around. I was really sick of him at this point. He would continue to have his buddies over to the house and they would still drink and eat everything we had. He and my mom were also about to get married. We were constantly at each other's throats. I would say to him, "Don't let your friends eat all of our food." He would yell, "Shut the fuck up!" I would yell right back at him. "This is my house, motherfucker. You shut the fuck up!" So when he came out front when I was wrestling with my friends, I knew something was up. He was looking for trouble. He had nothing to do while my mom was working all day and sometimes all night. Craig said he wanted to wrestle me and was kind of teasing me in front of my friends. "Come on, I'm not going to hurt you." Then he got down on his knees and was taunting me even more. "Come on, let's wrestle, you won't get hurt." It was getting uncomfortable and a little something inside me snapped. I charged him and clotheslined the mother-fucker. One hard shot across the head and he went down. Right away it looked like I hurt him. "You little sonofabitch, my back gave out!" He was pissed. He was flopping around on the ground and really seemed to be hurt. This wasn't going to go well. I figured the least I could do was help him back up. That's what I would've done if I had been messing around with my buddies, all of whom at this point could not believe what was going down. I gave him a hand and he took it. *Okay, maybe this will be okay*, I was thinking to myself at that point. But the next thing I knew, he popped right up. Motherfucker cold cocked me with a fist to the mouth. That motherfucker had set me up me. He wasn't hurt at all. He was just setting up a sucker punch—and a hard sucker punch at that. As pro wrestler Gorilla Monsoon might have said, he Pearl Harbored me. Total cheap shot. My friends were shocked. This was bad. I looked down and realized through all the blood gushing out of my mouth that he had knocked out my front teeth. I saw them on the ground, and I could fill the space in my mouth with my tongue. The warm blood and saliva were flowing out fast, so all my friends backed away at the same time, probably afraid they were going to get splattered on. Craig dusted himself off, pointed a finger at me, and barked, "Don't you say a word to your mother about what happened. Figure something else out." And then he walked back inside.

Damn. I needed a story as well as new teeth. I don't think I would've told her even if he didn't call me out like that. Deep inside I didn't want to hurt my mom. And she would've freaked out if she knew what really happened. So I just made up a story that I dove headfirst into a pool and missed. I just lied to her.

CHAPTER 7

Getting Up Off the Ground

This was an important moment for me. Craig had given me his best shot and I had gotten up. And everyone saw me get up. That made me tough in their eyes. My brother was panicked as usual. "You should've stayed down," he whispered to me. "He will hit you harder next time." I told my brother I wasn't going to live in fear. If he wanted to, he could do that. But that just wasn't how I lived my life. And that wasn't the end of it between me and Craig. I got my teeth fixed, but he was always looking at me like he wanted to punch them out again.

The next real showdown between him and me happened during a Nerf football game in our neighborhood. One thing I learned about Craig was that he was a wannabe athlete. He'd always yap about once having had a shot with the Red Sox, but I never believed him. But that's how he always fancied himself. He was always trying to prove himself with us kids, who were at least ten years younger than he was. Didn't matter to him. Always a lowlife. Anyway, back to the football game. Our neighborhood took these games seriously. It was a brother-hood. One street would play against another street. Two-hand touch. And we had rules. A crushed can was our first down marker, and we marched those yards off seriously to make a regulation-size field and everything, but all done with lots of sportsmanship and love. Everybody in the neighborhood looked forward to these games. It was like another big rite of passage. We based lots of friendships on these games, and they helped us develop a very special camaraderie from street to street. Well, Craig did not give a shit about any of that. He would insert himself into these games because he had nothing to do, and at one of these games, I scored a touchdown, and I saw him glaring at me. He was pissed. So on the kickoff, he blindsided me—crushed me into a parked car.

That was wrong. That was not how any of us rolled. I was hurt. My arm got numb quickly. All the other kids were looking at me like, "What the fuck is with this guy?" Everybody hated him. But he had nowhere to go and nothing to do. It turned out I bruised a bone in my arm pretty badly. As a result, one day in the house I spilled my cereal on the couch. I just couldn't handle the bowl right. It was my bad, though, and as I turned to go and clean up the mess I made, Craig kicked me in the back. He said that I was being disrespectful to him again. We had one of those heaters in the floor that blew hot air through a grate. Those damn things got hotter than hell, and if you ever stepped on it you felt like your foot was going to fall off. Well, I landed on that thing with my bad arm and to this day I still have that burn there. That scar still reminds me of the kind of hell this guy was making my life.

It sucked having that guy around. It just sucked. But my mom loved him. She pulled strings and got him a good job working with the city utility company. She even was able to get him enrolled in college—and everything was paid for. She knew everybody and she knew how the games were played. He started making good money, all because of my mom. All of that stuff was very hard for me to process. And then my mom got pregnant.

In a way, that was the worst thing that ever happened to me. Why? Because the news of her pregnancy turned me into a coward. My thinking was that when she has a baby, I wasn't going to matter anymore. I wasn't going to mean anything to her. And that stripped away all of my confidence and swagger. Other kids could smell it. I didn't fight anymore. I didn't stick up for anybody. I was just too scared. I would mutter something like, "My mama says I can't fight anymore." Which, of course, made kids want to fight me even more. My reputation at school started crumbling fast. I was no longer "that guy." It was really weird to feel that way. And it was all because of the pregnancy. My grades started to tank as well, which really sucked because I was a good student. Teachers liked me and I was focused. But even that started to fade.

Then my mom had a miscarriage. I'm not going to go into the details—they're simply too personal and graphic—but I was there for my mom when it happened. I helped her get through it and I watched what was going on, right up close. I comforted her as she cried, told her it was just nature's way, that everything would be okay. That strengthened and reinforced once more the bond with my mother. It was sort of like years earlier when I had gone after my father to protect her. That was another bonding moment for her and me. Craig, of course, made it seem like it was her fault. Like losing the baby was somehow on her. He was such a coward. I think she started to see what he was really about. But then she invited her parents, my grandparents, to help comfort her and get her through the whole miscarriage mess.

As usual, my grandfather wouldn't even look me in the eye, but my grandmother was as sweet and kind as ever. One night, I heard them all talking out in the living room. My mom was asking her dad his thoughts about her leaving Craig. She was getting fed up with him like I was. But her dad came down hard on her. "You can't get a divorce. You've been with a Black man before and actually had children with a Black man. The fact that any white man at all would have you now is a blessing." It's hard to even try and define his level of racism. I guess I can just say, it was pure and true. To him, race was every-thing. Black people were not just inferior; they were objects of shame.

I left the house after listening to that crap and was climbing a tree in the backyard when my grandmother came out. "George," she said, in that beautiful New England accent. "I know you're hurting and I only want to help you, so tell me, what can I do? What can I do for you?"

"Take me with you when you go home," I said. "Get me out of this place. I don't want to be here."

"I can't do that sweetheart. You know I can't do that." She frowned. "Your grandfather would never allow that. But you can always feel free to call me..."

No. At that point in my life, I had learned that telephone calls did nothing. They were no help. I appreciated the offer, but that's not what I wanted or needed. She gave me a hug and then brought me inside and made me one of her famous and wonderful grilled cheese sandwiches. And then she shared her Entenmann's cake with me. She really wanted me to feel better, and the fact that I was hurting really got to her, I could tell. But there was only so much she could do. After I finished eating, she came into my bedroom with a package for me. "I know it's your birthday in two days, but I want you to open this now, George." I unwrapped the package to discover a brand-new baseball glove. I gave her a big hug and said thank you. That was the only gift I got that birthday.

A couple of days later, I had a Little League game and my grandfather said, begrudgingly, that he would come to watch. As racist as he was, it still meant something to me to have him there. He and Craig got along incredibly well—which bothered me. At least if he came and watched me play then I could show him what I had. I could show him I was a decent kid who was a talented athlete and worked hard. I could see him sitting in the stands that day, glaring, expressionless. My next at-bat, I stepped to the plate. One of my best friends was on the mound throwing heat. Normally I would take the first pitch. All the players I liked, like Rich Gedman from the Red Sox, would take the first pitch—that is, let the first pitch go to see what the guy had. That's normally what I did. But not this time. That first pitch came in and I jacked it. Nobody was hitting home runs at that level of Little League that I was playing. But this thing sailed clear over the fence and then some. I got all of it. As I came around at second base and looked back toward the stands, I noticed that my grandfather had already left. He missed it. My heart sank. That was my chance to show him what I was made of, and he didn't even give me the courtesy of sticking around. Well, I just tried to shake it off. The coach gave me the game ball afterward and I brought it home, proud of myself.

CHAPTER 8

Craig Still Doesn't Get It

Life was not getting any easier. Soon after, my mom got pregnant again. I started getting those feelings of cowardice again and my grades were sinking even lower. But at least I made the PONY league baseball team. I was a solid right-field, first baseman, and occasional catcher. And I really loved baseball. Of course, this made Craig even crazier because he had always envisioned himself as a professional baseball player. My mom was working so much that it was on Craig to drop me off at practice and pick me up. But oftentimes he would never show up after a practice or even when the game was finished, and I would sit there till ten at night. When I was still in Little League, my mom was working so much, I remember the night the PONY League coach called me to tell me I had officially made the team. I was so happy. The coach went on to say that some of my grades needed to get better and that he would work with me and make sure I got the tutoring that I needed. I was happy to hear that he had faith in me. But before I could hang up with the coach, Craig grabbed the phone and said, "He's not playing baseball for you. He's disrespectful and his grades are not strong enough." That was the end of sports for me right then. My mom tried to intervene, but no dice. Craig had put his foot down and she was letting him get away with it.

He came home one day and my mom smelled perfume on him. He was definitely screwing around. She cried and I comforted her. He hated that because it made him look as bad as he was. So he came over to us and punched me in the stomach. Hard. That's when I started shedding the cowardice. I got up. It didn't hurt anymore. I thought to myself, *It's coming, you sonofabitch*. I felt it. I was becoming that reluctant hero I always dreamed of being. *It's coming, motherfucker*, I thought deep inside. And I think that was really when I started becoming a man.

So what to do next? No sports, bad grades—I didn't even have good enough grades to get into woodshop. Well, I got approached by Mr. Rivera, the drama teacher. He thought I was funny. He'd say, "Get up in front of class and tell five jokes." I would pull from my Richard Pryor repertoire and crack everyone up. Mr. Rivera made a difference in my life. He got me involved in drama class. I auditioned and got a part in the show *Drift to New York*. Drama? Who knew? Mr. Rivera was a big, strong guy. Powerful. We all thought he was gay because he was the head of the drama department. Plus, he was very sensitive and seemed soft. Well, one night after rehearsal he took us all to Shakey's Pizza and his wife was there. You know what a ten is. This lady was a twelve. I think she sensed what we were thinking about him and she said to us, "Gentlemen, he is all man, a true stud," and she held her hands out to illustrate just how big he was. Well, now this guy became like a god to us. He really helped me believe in myself and helped me develop my outward personality. I was in the ninth grade at that point, which was when things got pretty awkward in terms of growth, hormones, emotions, and the like, but he stuck by me and even had me enter the school talent show. I got up there and killed. The vice-principal pulled me aside and said, "You know what, son? You are going to be on television someday. You've got a lot of personality and a lot of talent."

That made me feel good because I was basically spending most of my time by myself; by that point my mom had had the baby (and had another one on the way) and that's where her time was spent. Craig had cut his thumb splitting wood with an ax one night while he was attempting to cut the stump off of our Christmas tree, and so, of course, my mom stepped up and got him a desk job that paid better and had great benefits. This was one lucky motherfucker, this guy.

And then we moved again.

Moving to Palmdale was another new, big step in life. It was very different from Sunland-Tujunga. It was the high desert. Much more barren and remote. At least Sunland was sort of part of Los Angeles, but Palmdale was like going to another planet. Everything was remote and isolated. But my grandparents had helped finance a house out there for my mom and Craig because prices were cheaper and she was looking to make a move. For me, it was tough. We had been at the last place for a couple of years, which for us was a long time. I had made good friends. I even had a girlfriend at that point. It was tough saying goodbye to everybody. I had just a few days to get it all together, and then boom! we would be gone. The thing with me was, I was conditioned to not make many plans for the future. I didn't say "Goodbye, we will stay in touch," or anything like that. I had been taught that goodbye meant goodbye and that was that. No phone calls, no nothing. And so off we went.

Soon my mom had not one but two little babies with Craig and her hands were full. I was once again going to play sports, so I joined the football team at school. I had grown to six foot five and was developing lots of muscles. I was becoming a beast. And pretty quickly I found a new girlfriend, a pretty, white Italian girl, and this was really my first experience with a woman. As far as the racial makeup of the school, it was mostly white, but there were also plenty of Mexicans and Blacks. Everybody pretty much got along, especially when it came down to sports. No real tensions as far as race went—at least, that I was aware of. I do remember that when the movie *Malcolm X* came out, a lot of us Brothers embraced it and really got in touch with our Blackness.

There was a guy at my new school named Mr. Ray, a Southern, white teacher, and he really taught me about respecting my heritage and embracing a true work ethic. Mr. Ray was a Southern gentleman if there ever was one. He was my US history teacher in high school—tenth grade, I believe. He had a Southern drawl when telling the story of US history, which really drew us in. Mr. Ray gave the class an assignment: what would we do or where would we go if we could go back in time and change US history? I knew just what to write about! That was the greatness of Mr. Ray. He made learning fun and we looked forward to what we were talking about in class. There were discussions, debates; it was all good. Mr. Ray loved what he did and it spread to the classroom. So, getting back to it, for my assignment I wrote an essay that scholars could hold up to some of the greatest literature ever known; it was impactful, controversial, and, dare I say...brilliant! I wrote that I'd go back and tell the Native Americans the whites were coming and that Thanksgiving was a trap, and that they should keep Pocahontas away from John Smith and unite against their enemy! I turned in my paper with a certain arrogance— or maybe bravado! I figured Mr. Ray surely would read it to the class or submit it to the Smithsonian for review, right? I was so excited about my paper. His class was fifty-five minutes long, but it was an escape from a bad home life. Mr. Ray took the top three stories and let the class vote. I made the cut! And he did indeed read the stories to the class.

When mine came up, he read it with a smirk but respected the basic message of the story. Then when it came to voting he said, "Okay. Who wants to vote for Mr. Murdoch's story of having all the Native Americans come together and kill all the white people?" The class laughed but I didn't get the votes I felt I deserved for this epic story. I went to Mr. Ray after and said, "I guess I didn't think about the killing..."

He said, "Well, to be honest, you don't speak any Native American, do you?"

I said, "No."

"Well, I think we are all safe then." He then said, "I heard you're going through some things at home."

I explained to him how miserable I was at home and how bad the situation with Craig was, how I had nothing really positive to keep me occupied.

Mr. Ray said, "Well I've got some work around my front and backyard if you're looking to earn some money."

I said, "Yes, sir!"

The next weekend, I got dropped off at Mr. Ray's house and we worked all damned day, laying sod for his backyard, digging up tree roots and rocks and doing basic landscaping. All in the hot sun. We broke for lunch and his wife made a Southern feast: fried chicken, mashed potatoes, and a bunch of other stuff. It was Thanksgiving, damn near. We worked until sunset and then he handed me fifty dollars. "Come back tomorrow and we'll finish up," he said.

That money meant the world to me. I earned it; I worked hard and I did it right! Something about a hard day's work really appealed to me. Mr. Ray said, "Son, no matter what happens in life, they can never take away your work ethic. Only you can do that. Starting at the bottom is no problem if you're not afraid of the work and the commitment to improving yourself. Hard work always pays off. Always." I've never forgotten that lesson. It lives with me today, thanks to a Southern gentleman named Mr. Ray—a man who took the time to make a difference. Whenever I do that today with a young person, I think of him.

In California, high school began in the tenth grade, and things were looking up for me. I was making new friends, was getting started in football, and my grades were starting to climb back up. Maybe I was just growing up, but things were beginning to settle a bit. I was looking ahead and just becoming a man. I should've figured things would not stay the course for long. But sometimes nature does take its course. Earthquakes happen, volcanoes erupt. It's just part of the natural cycle. It's not a bad thing; it just has to happen so that the growth of the planet can continue. You never know when something big is gonna go down. BIG. Pivotal. A game changer. You're just moving along the coil, minding your own business, then BAM.

One night my family and I were all having dinner. The phone rang. My mom was pregnant again at that point. Craig answered the phone. It was my girlfriend, evidently. "Listen," he said to her, "We are eating. You don't call here between five and seven p.m., do you understand? Better yet, how about don't ever call here again, you little slut."

That was the lightning bolt. Hearing him talk to my girl like that in front of my family was all it took for me to lose control. In a way, my entire life had been building up to that single moment. I took a spoonful of mashed potatoes and threw it in Craig's face. My brother laughed. Even my mom was suppressing a little chuckle. He stood up, but not with his usual confidence. There I was, standing six foot five, 270 pounds. He realized that might be a problem; he looked at my mother and said, "He can't do that." That was interesting. At one time he would've stared me down, but now he was looking at my mother.

"Bro," I said. "Why are you talking to your wife? I'm right here."

He didn't want to engage with me. "Let's go outside," he said to me.

Time to pay your bill, I thought to myself. *Is he shaking?*

He got up and slowly made his way toward the door, muttering to me, "I fight dirty, you know. Remember, I fight dirty."

I knew that. And I knew what was coming. The second we got out to the back patio, out of the corner of my eye I saw his punch coming toward the side of my head and I simply turned and I caught it. I caught it with my bare hand. And then I reached back, and in my mind was all of my years of hatred, anger, and aggravation, and I hit him so hard that I think he flew about five feet back. His feet went over his head. That was it. Everything inside me was about to unleash. I calmly walked over, grabbed him by his neck, and dragged him over to the rose garden wooden gazebo-thing he had so proudly built when we first moved in. I then threw him against the wood and it smashed. I started pummeling him with lefts and rights. He had no recourse. I was just too overpowering. I shattered his orbital socket and I saw his fingers start twitching. He started pleading with me, but I didn't care. My brother came out and tried pulling me back, saying, "George, you'll go to jail. I don't want you to go to jail!" My mother was crying and I finally exhausted myself. He was hurt badly. I couldn't help myself. I thought about all the humiliation he had exposed me to over the years. I thought of how he badly he'd treated my mother. I thought of when he knocked my teeth out. Honestly, I didn't care what happened to this motherfucker in this moment. My mother did, though, and she had already called the cops when it started. Within minutes a sheriff's car screeched up in front of the house along with an ambulance full of paramedics. The sheriff calmly asked what was going on. Craig could barely breathe but he managed to say to the guy, "I asked him to step outside."

"Wait," the sheriff said. "You challenged him? Challenged a minor? That changes the rules right there."

Craig was the one in the wrong. By law, an adult can't challenge a minor to fight.

"He's the new king of the mountain," Craig kept muttering to the cop. Bitch, please. *You were never king of the mountain. You were never even governor of the hill. You're not in a position to declare me anything*, I was thinking.

I really appreciated the sheriff. He pulled me aside and said, "Son, do you have somewhere to go? I think you need to get out of here. I can tell this is not a healthy environment for you. I want you to relax, clean up, put some stuff in the back, and go stay with a friend for now."

So that's what I did.

CHAPTER 9

The Next Chapter in Life

I packed a trash bag with a bunch of clothes and that night I slept in the locker room at school. For pretty much my entire high school experience—the next two years—I was a couch surfer, staying with friends, however I could get it done. It was never easy. I was a big guy and I took up a lot of space. Thankfully, I had good friends. I didn't talk to my mom throughout most of my high school days because of what happened that night. My situation didn't really allow for a normal existence. I went to my classes and I did the work. But there wasn't much fun. No proms or parties. For me, it was all about getting by, making sure I had a place to crash. That was my life. My buddy's father, kind of the team dad for football, reached out to me and told me he had invited my mother to come to graduation. He was such a good man and he really stuck his neck out. He told me she was going to be there.

Well, graduation day rolled around and I didn't see my mother in the chair that had been saved. What broke my heart was she'd made this man a liar. He didn't care. He hugged me and kissed me on the cheek just like he did his own son. This was a real man. He knew how to show love. Would I ever be like that? That's what I wanted. That man made a real impression on me.

With graduation over, I had the rest of my life staring at me right in the face. What the hell was I going to do? Then, one day, the phone rang. Somebody had tracked me down. It was the coach of the local junior college. "I need a lineman. Someone like you."

I didn't have a plan. I mean, I had been couch surfing for literally two years. Totally on my own, not having any real idea what the next day was going to be like. A week on your own is a lot of time. Think about two years. I was afraid to look a day ahead at times. It was just too scary. A lot of nights I would lie wherever I was, my heart beating like I had run the hundred-yard dash, overhearing my friend's parents talking about when I needed to go. Everybody was really generous, up to a point. I knew deep inside that I was an interruption to their lives. They could give me a place to sleep for maybe a couple of weeks, but then it would start getting weird. I got it. It was hard. I was the big puppy in the window that looked cute until you brought it home. Then the shit got real.

So by the time this guy named Coach Martinez reached out to me, I was just avoiding as much reality as I could. I had been through a lot in my life at that point for my age, and I didn't have the luxury of living for the moment. I was all about, where would I be spending the next night? There wasn't a lot of time for fun or the reckless irresponsibility that goes with youth. So when a coach from Antelope Valley College wanted to talk to me about playing football for his team, the Marauders, I was very interested, knowing I didn't have many options.

Coach Martinez was an interesting guy. Very down-to-earth, big thick glasses and dark curly hair that looked like it was permed, but I was never really sure. He was Mexican but he was also Mormon, which was an interesting combination. We met, we hit it off pretty well, and he gave me a summer-time schedule for practice.

That was a good opportunity for me. He had heard good things about me and seemed excited about having me on the squad. I didn't drive or anything so I figured I would just borrow a bicycle when practices started. I still wasn't talking to my mom so I had nobody to fall back on, even in terms of hitching a ride here or there. I really was by myself once high school ended. Once practices began and I met my first college football buddies, I felt right away like I had a little bit of a community. These were dudes that came from all over the place and we seemed to have a lot in common just in terms of being independent and self-motivated.

I'll tell you what, it wasn't easy. Our first sessions began with jogs through the high desert—which were pretty brutal. Coach Martinez was all about footwork in addition to running through sand, and he had us jumping a lot of rope as well. We wanted to play football and couldn't quite figure out why this is so important. We were very green in that respect. High school football had been all about football. None of this esoteric training regarding footwork or anything like that. You were basically always out on the field running drills and practicing plays. That said, I embraced everything because I trusted and respected Coach Martinez. He was a good man, and since I had no place else to go, I spent a lot of time at the gym. I was there every day during the summer, lifting weights all the time—so I was getting much stronger. The 220 test was the most brutal. We had to run down around the goalposts and back in thirty-seven seconds. It just sucked. Every single day—like twelve times—he would push us to do that drill. And you have to understand, the air in the high desert is very dry and you get winded very easily. But it was molding me. The intense discipline with shaping me. It was all good.

Then I also had to get ready to go to school. This wasn't just about football. So Coach Martinez helped me figure out the registration process and it made the transition to junior college a lot easier. I still didn't have any money, but the classes were only about fifty bucks per credit and some of my friends' parents were helping me. I was always flat broke. I mean, if everybody was going out for a burger, I would often skip it because I couldn't even afford that. To get certain courses, I needed ACT and SAT scores, but I had skipped the tests in high school. So I just basically made up scores, nothing too crazy, maybe 735 or so (which was well within the realm of reality), and no questions were asked. In addition to my friends helping me out with a couple of hundred bucks here or there to pay for classes and supplies, some special arrangement was worked out behind the scenes between the coaches and the school administrators. Everything would be taken care of for me that I needed. Look, athletes are always going to get the long end of the stick. It may not be fair but it's just the way it is.

In high school, race was no big deal, but at junior college there was definitely some segregation going on; however, all of it was self-administered. That is to say, the Brothers from California hung out together, the Brothers from Florida hung out together, and so on. Geography had seemed to be driving together the little cliques that were forming.

We linemen bonded right away because that's just the most thankless job in the world when it comes to football. No glamour, no credit, no nothing. When things go right, everybody else gets the glory. When things fall apart, you are the first ones they come looking for. But we got along great and formed our own little linebacker community, which I really valued. In terms of personal relationships then, I didn't have much going on. There was no time for romance or anything; it was all about getting my schoolwork done and practice, practice, practice. I strategically organized my week based on food. For instance, Thursday at practice was pizza day so I would grab as many extra slices as I could and make that last until Monday. I would load up wherever I could and whenever I could like a squirrel, stashing away as much food as I would need for the next few days.

One thing I was learning as we developed as a unit was just how important teamwork is. It was like you guys against the world. I liked that sense that I could lean on these guys and they could lean on me. In high school, it wasn't that organized. It was pretty much everybody out for themselves. But junior college was a different experience and it was helping me a great deal. Coach Martinez continued being a very good influence on me. He never raised his voice, but he was still very intense and he got the job done. Everybody respected him. I was learning from him, too, about how to get along with people. I was also becoming like the ambassador on the team. I could roll with the Florida Brothers, the California Brothers...I was the guy that could move group to group and get along with everybody. I sensed that was important because it helped build leadership skills.

Another thing Coach Martinez stressed was the importance of being a well-rounded man. He would say, "I would sacrifice a great football player for a well-rounded man." And I took that to heart. But I know he also had concerns about me. I could be a smart-ass and I could be very outspoken. I could start a lot of shit, and I could come off as an angry Black guy with no direction. I was mercurial. I was coming from a lot of different places, but I was trying too hard to pull it all together. Coach was patient with me, though. He never gave up on me. And he pushed me. He wanted to see me press three hundred pounds in the weight room but I couldn't do it. I was actually nervous about failure, so I stayed away from the weight room. I didn't want to be seen as weak. But he got me there. "Let me see what you got," he would say to me. And I would do what I could do and he would say, "You can do more than that. You're a strong kid; you can do more than that." I believed him and he pushed me and made me believe I could do more and finally, I pressed three hundred.

I had a good first season. I was starting to settle in and then I did something stupid. One of the guys on the team, a big white kid named Joe who reminded me of Hoss on the TV show *Bonanza*, heard about an opportunity up north at Contra Costa Junior College. Something about if you had a good season up there, they could get you right to a Division I school, which is what all of us were thinking about. That's what it was about: getting to Division I. I literally packed my stuff up once the season was over and headed up north to start summer practice sessions at a new place. I didn't talk to my coaches; I just split. It was a shitty thing to do given all the time and energy they had put into me. But I was still something of a wild animal. I wasn't polished and I wasn't always disciplined when it came to my personal behavior. I saw an opportunity and I just jumped at it. Not cool. We got up there, met the coach; he found us an apartment and we were just living off of Top Ramen as we started practicing. Joe got bored and went back down south soon afterward, leaving me high and dry, which sucked. So I knew what I had to do. I had to beg my way back with Coach Martinez. I called to see if he would let me back on the team and he said to me, "No promises, but let's see what we can do. One thing you should do is contact your mother, Tyrus."

My coach wanted me to reunite with my family. Family was as important to Coach Martinez as it was to his coaching style. He saved my life. It was his teaching and coaching that stuck with me even though I may not have appreciated it at the time. He worked the team so hard and with discipline. We did the running back drills plus our own defensive drills. We never walked on grass, always "on the hop," as he said. I still do it today subconsciously—on the hop! You could never just walk. He ran with us, lifted with us, spent hours molding men. He took us to the movies, and we went to the Green Burrito to see if we could eat the giant burrito. He was so much more than just a coach. And even with all my family issues, he wanted me to make amends with my mother, not even knowing our history. I never talked about it. Asking my mom if I could move home for the football season sucked, but worse was asking one of our other coaches, Coach Carter, to let me come back to the team. Coach Carter had stone-white hair, a red face, and was the toughest coach of the team. He demanded respect, accountability, and no excuses. There was a game once where we had gotten into a shoving match with another team. They weren't coached like us. I saw the fight brewing and started heading toward it! Like a lion to a kill. Half the rosters were ready. Coach turned to us and said, "If one of you steps one foot on this field, I will haunt you for the rest of your days. No scholarship, no job, I'll be there." Remember in *Tombstone* when Wyatt Earp put the gun to Ike's head and some dummy said, "Let's rush him, he's bluffing"? And Ike, in the gentlest words, said, "No, he ain't bluffing." The entire offense looked like that! We took a knee as instructed! When I wanted to return to the Marauders, I had to face Coach Carter and ask for a second chance. Coach Martinez could have called my mom for me, talked to Coach Carter for me, but he was teaching me to become a man. Up until that point, I had almost no reference about how to behave like a man. And when I asked Coach Carter to come back to the team, he looked at me, stern, and said, "How's your grades?"

I said, "Good, coach."

"Did you pass summer school?" he asked.

"Yes, sir."

"I got a call from a Mr. Lacy. He was impressed with your work ethic and you got all Bs. You will not start for me. I don't trust you. But you can try and make the team."

I said, "Thank you, sir."

He said, "Don't thank me, show me!"

Now, during that time in Lodi, California, while I was attending Contra Costa, all I had was schoolwork to do. Schoolwork and watching Peg Bundy. But I took an African-American history class with Mr. Lacy. He challenged me, told me to question and research everything. What is Black? What is pretty? Why is the picture of a blond, white woman on a billboard? He was a strong Black man with frosted white hair; he was dark and short, but had the strongest voice. He made me look at myself. Once, after about two weeks of two-a-day practices in the high desert heat, Coach Carter said to me as I jogged by, "I talked to Professor Lacy and it looks like we made the right choice! You're back on first team!"

Coach Martinez described me as the most trash-talking, nonstop big mouth on the field, but he also thought I was clever and entertaining out there. But he knew that was my confidence—real confidence that he had instilled in me—making me face fear and using it to be better!

CHAPTER 10

Nebraska

As far as reacclimating back at home, it was strange at first. My mother, while happy to see me, was also on guard. Of course, she could not forget the beating that I had delivered on her husband. But like she told me, she was still my mother, she missed me, and she wanted to at least establish some sort of relationship again. As far as Craig, that dynamic was completely different when I moved back in. I had done a lot of thinking about the situation with him while I had been away and something came to my mind. When he would come at me over the years, when he would attack me, he knew where and how to hit me. It was pretty obvious to me that he had been through much of the same things growing up. He was obviously a victim of child abuse, in my opinion. I brought it up with my mother a couple of times; I could tell she did not want to talk about it, but her reactions validated the premise. And so Craig and I, while never getting close, of course, could at least tolerate each other now. He'd become very docile, very submissive around me. By now, they were raising their two kids, my brother was still in the picture, and, overall, things were going well for them. But that was all because of how hard my mother was working. As I soon learned once moving back in, over the years she had done whatever she could to help finance his dreams. She had invested and lost a lot of money in a baseball card shop. Other small businesses had gone bust as well after my mom had made her investments. At the time I came back, Craig had gotten into boating. He wanted to be a professional fisherman. So my mom had refinanced the house as a way of buying him not one, but two, boats. He would go to fishing tournaments all over the place while she continued to work her ass off and also raise two young kids.

Craig was still trying to act like a big shot, but he had really done nothing on his own. And his cavalier attitude actually got in my way when I received a letter from Washington State University, which was interested in perhaps having me come play football for them. Craig had gone ahead and answered the letter himself and, when it came time to fill out financial portions, he wrote in the box he was making $250,000. He was lying, of course, trying to be a big man, and that grotesque inaccuracy cost me a scholarship at least. This was the guy who obviously was always going to be getting in my way, even if it didn't involve the physical beatings.

Not long after I got home, my mom told me that she thought Craig was having an affair. I went into protection mode, of course. That's something that would always happen with me and my mom. Evidently, he had come home with lipstick and perfume on his shirt, and rather than throwing it out or getting it cleaned, he stuck it at the bottom of the hamper. Really stupid. My mom found the shirt and told me what she thought was going on. She didn't want me to do anything, she just needed to talk. Still, I confronted him, and he was scared when he saw that old look in my eyes. But my mother didn't want me to do anything. He made up some story to her about having hugged the secretary at work—and my mom bought it. It was weird. My mom needed me when she needed to talk and get things off her chest; that's when I would be her hero. But when she gave in to whatever Craig wanted, then I just got in the way again. Some things never changed.

When Washington State realized there was fraudulent information on my submission form, I got in trouble and had to sit out for a year of eligibility as a red shirt. No Division I school was going to take me now. But then I got an offer from University of Nebraska at Kearney—a full-ride scholarship. They didn't care about what had happened on the application. They wanted me and so I packed my backpack and hit the road.

They flew me out to Nebraska. I honestly think my mom was happy to see me go. She would miss me when I was gone, but when I'd come back, she always seemed ready for me to leave again. Just after I arrived in Nebraska, I went to a welcome mixer party at the local Holiday Inn. It was literally my first day there. A good-looking girl approached me and I told her I liked the tattoo on her leg. She said to me, "Hey I have a tattoo on my pussy as well. Would you like to see?"

Are you kidding? "You bet," I told her.

In the background, her boyfriend was getting furious. He came right over to me and said, "Maybe you just get a tattoo on your pussy as well."

There we went. I looked him in the eye and said, "Hey, I have a dick; that's why she's hitting on me."

He said, "Oh really, wise guy?" This was a white guy we're talking about. In Nebraska. He said, "I've got backup here with my buddies, so you better be careful." So I did what I was used to doing when confronted like this: I hauled back and laid him out with one punch. And then all hell broke loose. I got hit in the head with a plate before one of my friends that I just met there, another Black football player, grabbed me and dragged me out of the place. As I was leaving, I heard one of the white guys yell, "That's right, go back to the jungle!"

Are you fucking kidding me? When I got back to the dorm, I said to the rest of my Brothers, "That white boy let loose with a pretty bad racist slur." That's all these guys needed to hear. We went off to find him. One of the guys knew the frat house where they lived. We knocked on the door and, as soon as it opened, we busted in. I saw the guy that made that racist crack to me, and, as I pulled back to punch him, my elbow cracked right into the face of the girl with the tattoo who started this whole mess. It was a total accident, and I felt horrible as my elbow hit her chin. She got very upset, and I was being as apologetic as I could. The sheriffs showed up almost immediately and ran us all down to the local jail. One of the cops said to me, "You're that big kid from California, right?" I nodded quietly. "Don't make this a habit okay, son?" And he let me go. I appreciated him letting me off. But now I had a reputation.

At another party shortly after I arrived in Nebraska—one I didn't get in a fight at—I met my first real girlfriend, Amber. She was a pretty white girl, very innocent, and she worked with the trainers and the football team taping ankles and things like that. She was lovely and had a calming influence on me. I had no skills with women at that point so I would just tell jokes to make her laugh. We left that party together that same night.

"What kind of car you drive?" she asked me.

"My shoes," I chuckled. "I don't have a car."

Later that night, we were watching TV in my dorm room and she stood up over me and said, "Okay, let's get this over with."

I wasn't sure what she meant. She started taking her top off and I said, "Wait, aren't we just going to watch a movie?"

She stopped and looked at me, surprised. She completely stopped what she was doing and laid down with me on my bed, and we just watched a movie and then fell asleep together.

When we woke up the next morning she looked at me and said, "Thank you."

"For what?" I said.

She explained that she had dated another Black athlete before me, and, evidently, he had forced her to have sex. This was an entirely different experience for both of us. I was still a virgin at that point and I was awkward when it came to girls. But I liked Amber a lot right from the beginning. There was something special about her.

Once the season got going and I settled into school, I really got to like Nebraska. It was a pretty, calm, and reasonable place. I liked my teammates; we played well together and I was starting to settle down as a young man. A few weeks into the season, my mom said she wanted to come visit, which I thought was a great idea, but when she arrived, I was shocked to see that she had brought Craig with her. I shouldn't have been too surprised, I guess; I mean, they were married, for God's sake. But I just didn't want him involved in my life at all, and I was disappointed in my mom for bringing him along. It was an awkward visit overall and it was the only time she ever came to see me in Nebraska. Amber's parents came out for the same game, which was homecoming, but that became a problem. Right before they came over to her dorm room, she started explaining to me nervously that I couldn't meet them because they would have a problem with my skin color. That depressed me.

As she explained her anxiety, there was a knock at the door in her dorm. They had arrived earlier than expected and we didn't know what to do. She had a waterbed, and if you know what those things are like, there's hardly any room to hide underneath, but she told me I had to disappear so I managed somehow to squeeze under that thing. I could see everyone's feet from under the bed. What really killed me was the conversation that I was eavesdropping on. They were asking her all about some guy back home. About her life back there. Clearly she had other things going on that I did not know about and, all of a sudden, I was unsure about where I fit into her life. It was crushing because I knew we would never be able to be normal in front of her family. When they finally left—after more than *five* hours—I squeezed out from under the bed. Amber was heartbroken and embarrassed. We both felt sick to our stomachs, but I didn't handle it well. That moment of feeling shamed by her family, being forced under her bed, changed things dramatically. Things were never quite the same with Amber after that experience. I would start cheating on her soon. It made me resent white people even more than I did already. I should've broken up with her right there and then but I didn't. I just dragged her along for a while and did whatever else I wanted.

Between my stepdad, grandfather, Amber's dad—all of these white men in my life combined to make me angry. I started copping a real attitude at school. I got angrier and angrier and was pissing my coaches off with my behavior. I also started becoming depressed. I was very unsure of myself, and I was tired of being treated in certain ways. I decided to get back at Amber by sleeping with as many white girls as I could. But that wasn't the answer to anything.

CHAPTER 11

The Road to the WWE

Me and my buddy Bink Vasean had all kinds of plans. We were going to start a nightclub called Atmosphere. We were going to be rappers. But the thing we really wanted to do was to become wrestlers. We wanted to form a tag team that would change the world. We found an ad for a "wrestling college" up in Canada that was run by an old former wrestler named Ike "the Crippler" Shaw. It was called the Von Erich-Hart Brothers School of Wrestling and was located in Cambridge, Ontario. The ad said the wrestling school had trained Edge, Christian, Rhyno, Test, Just Joe, Glenn Kulka, and Laura Bennett. In addition, they had promoted events with the Bushwhackers, King Kong Bundy, and Tito Santana. They were set up to train twenty-four wrestlers who lived on-site and six more off-site. The school had a ring available in the evenings, seven days a week, and a twenty-four-hour, seven-days-a-week gym available for students.

Bink thought the place had a good website; we looked up the link and sent them our pictures, and they told us to come on up because they could help us get in the WWE. Now, in my head, I thought this was going to be like a real college, with a campus and dorm rooms and everything. We were so excited when we got in Bink's car and drove up there. We were daydreaming the whole way, imagining what it was going to be like when we both got to perform in WrestleMania. It was exciting.

Until we got there.

The place was a fucking joke. Ike was basically Mr. Krabs from *SpongeBob*. He was short and cranky and always used the word "cocksucker." Started every other sentence with it. The dorms were basically closets with bunk beds and we literally could wrestle only at night because the bank next door would complain about all the noise that was going on. Ike had all kinds of autographs on the wall that me and Bink thought made him legit, not realizing that anybody could go out and collect autographs and put framed pictures on the wall. The only thing about him that was really impressive was the amount of cologne that he wore, some sort of industrial-strength, heavy-duty perfume that he basically covered himself in. Obviously, Ike "the Crippler" Shaw didn't seem to be in any position to make all of our wrestling dreams come true. But while we were there, we went through the courses for a couple of weeks to try to make the best of it. But the whole thing just fell like a scam. That said, he did send us to the WWE office in Toronto after claiming he made an appointment for us.

When I got to the WWE offices in Toronto, I didn't feel great. I was nervous and I also had a pretty bad flu. I felt out of place, as well. I mean, walking into the lobby in my letterman jacket didn't seem like a very WWE look. *Is this place even legit?* I wondered when I walked in. Well, there was a poster of the Undertaker, so that was a good sign. Admittedly, however, I was thrown when I saw the secretary sitting behind the desk in the front office. She was dressed in head-to-toe leather. Not exactly business attire. Not to judge, but it just seemed a little bit strange. She asked who I was and I told her that I was a wrestler who was there to meet a guy named Carl. She laughed at me. Not a flirty laugh. A sarcastic laugh. A snicker. As if she was saying, "You?" Who the hell was she to be judging me like this? Either way, it pushed my anxiety further into the red zone. Maybe I didn't belong here. She eventually led me into Carl's office and right away he struck me as a very confident guy. He gave me a brief rundown of his background and then sat back in his chair, paused, and said, "So why are you here today?" I explained to him that the person in Ontario (Ike) had told me that he (Carl) had seen a video of me working out and wanted me to come here to the office in Toronto.

Carl gave me the kind of look that the secretary had given me out in the lobby. "Not true," he said. "That didn't happen." *Oh.* He continued. "You really want to be in this business? You really think you've got what it takes to be WWE caliber?" He didn't even really give me time to finish an answer. "Look at you," he said. "Your look is so confusing. You're not really Black, but you're also not really white. I don't get what you are."

"What about The Rock?" I asked.

"Look," he said. "The Rock is The Rock. You are not The Rock, okay? But thanks for stopping by."

There was nothing redeeming about this meeting. Nothing at all to "put in the bank" as they say. It was a long drive back to Nebraska. I was seriously crushed. The whole thing felt like a setup. I regretted the entire episode. I knew it was going to be something that I just blanked out of my mind and tried to forget about. But, unfortunately, those are the things that tend to eat away at you.

CHAPTER 12

Back from Atlanta

Without going into too much detail because I really don't feel like implicating people in this book, I once again in my life got totally screwed over after making an ill-advised drive to Atlanta. Another wild shot at making some money, another stupid and reckless shot at some kind of "immortality" I guess I was in search of. We were taking what I call a "penitentiary chance" on this drug run, money stuffed in the two spare tires in the back of a Suburban and everything, thinking it was going to be a great payoff. But it didn't happen. Once we got down there, our connection told us flat out, "You're going to make double next one. Just know that. But there's nothing for you here right now."

Once again, a bunch of promises that led to nothing. It made me just think that everything was bullshit. I was led to believe over and over there was a pot of gold at the end of the rainbow, but it turned out over and over to be just a pot of shit. I felt stupid and I felt angry. So what were we going to do about it? We drove back to Southern California, and I resumed my now well-oiled habit of crashing on other people's couches until I finally got up the nerve to ask my mom if she could help finance a trip back to Nebraska so I could finish school. Thankfully, she was happy to do it, so she bought my plane ticket and had already called the school to set me up with a dorm room. I really appreciated that. That was one thing about my mom. For everything we'd been through, she definitely stepped up a number of times and I'll always be very grateful for that.

One thing she couldn't change, though, was what it felt like to be back in Nebraska. I was just plain defeated. It was important for me to go back and finish school, but I still had no plans and being back there I just felt like a failure. Nothing was working out. The idea in my head was just to go back, hit the books, lay low, and finish up. Get on with my life. But there is something about selling drugs. Once you've done it for a while, it seems to find you wherever you are. I didn't go back to Nebraska to sell drugs. If anything, I wanted a fresh start. But it found me.

I was taking a full class load and a friend of mine said, "Hey, I've got a good connection in California. He can get us blocks of Mexican Red Hair weed," which is basically dirt weed, or just plain shit. The funny thing is, dirt weed in Los Angeles is chronic in Nebraska. People on the West Coast are so spoiled, but in Nebraska this was a pretty big deal. We broke the blocks up and sold it around town in a variety of sizes from ounces all the way down to dime bags. I hate to say it, but the money was good. Between us we would clear five or six grand over a weekend. I had money in my pocket, I could buy nice clothes, and I could eat semidecent food. I just couldn't embrace the whole thing, though, because I didn't want that lifestyle to define me. There was a time I would've been really offended if somebody had come up to me and said,

"I want to buy some weed," because I did not want to be that guy. But when I returned to Nebraska, there I was—that guy. I was a petty drug dealer.

Things were going well enough that our business expanded beyond just weed. My friend started bringing shrooms, and then, worst of all, crack cocaine. My business was dealing it, but I was never doing any of it personally. It just wasn't my thing. The suppliers that would come to our apartment would let us sample things if we wanted to, but I wanted no part of that. The reason I was so scared of cocaine went back to the death of basketball star Len Bias. I was a die-hard Celtics fan growing up and Len Bias was going to be the next Michael Jordan. I was so excited the day he was drafted in 1986. I had read all about him and I really liked his style. Lots of Celtic fans were excited. But when I got home from school one day my mom had the TV on. I watched the news reports about his death. He had done cocaine, and it killed him. I cried like I had lost my best friend. He had such an impact on me. I knew after that I would never touch cocaine. Not after what it did to Len Bias.

So there I was in this shitty little part of Nebraska, and people were bringing cocaine and crack and everything else around me and they were showing us how the business worked. They demonstrated how to prep the drugs, how to sell the drugs, and how to take the drugs. I knew nothing about that shit; yet. To help, I started chopping some cocaine up on the table with a razor blade and got some on my hand. One of the dealers lost his mind. "What the fuck are you doing? If it gets on your fingers it will get in your system!" He was scaring the crap out of me, and I was running around the room screaming, "How do I get this shit off my hand? Get this shit off of me, motherfucker!" And they got even more pissed off 'cause I was knocking the shit on the floor. I was making a mess and blowing lots of money right before their eyes. Clearly, I was not a good drug dealer.

There was one time I did experiment a little bit by trying something. I did shrooms one night at a buddy's place. Some friends were playing dominoes and I didn't really want to, but they all put a little bit in some tea and we all drank it. There was lots of peer pressure that night to try it. I was starting to get nervous, thinking, *What if I lose my mind?* Thankfully, nothing happened. At least right away. Those guys kept saying, "Don't worry, mushrooms are fun. They can't hurt you. They expand your mind. You going to like this." But nothing was happening.

We put on the television, another hour went by, and I felt totally normal. There was a painting on the wall with a guy fishing in a river. One of the guys in the room said to me, "George, come on, you better take your shoes off." I asked him why and he said, "Your feet are going to get wet from that river." We all started laughing because we realized that he believed the river was actually flowing through the room. Before too long, I started seeing exactly what he was saying. The river fucking came alive and it was flowing right over my feet; I could feel the fucking water. It was the strangest thing I've ever experienced. Everybody was laughing hard because we were all feeling the same thing. It was weird. It wasn't really that scary, but it was nothing I wanted to do again. I woke up the next morning and it felt like somebody had shoveled dirt into my mouth. I tried spitting it out into the sink, but the feeling wouldn't go away. I caught my reflection in the mirror and I looked like shit. I looked tired. I looked unhealthy.

By that time, I had started carrying a pistol because I was worried about getting robbed. Word got around what was going on at our apartment and lots of girls would turn up. One of them, a good-looking girl I had been aware of from a couple of years earlier, got really mad at me one night. Copped a serious attitude.

"What's wrong with you?" I asked her.

"What's wrong with *me*? You walk around this town like you own it. You're not shit. You're a drug dealer. You used to have shit going on. You're an athlete. There's people that looked up to you. And look at you now. You're just a no-good drug dealer."

Then she left. The homeboys in the house were like, "Fuck her, don't listen to her." But her words stung. I knew what she was saying, and she was right. I was a goddamn drug dealer. I started thinking, *This is not LA, this is Nebraska. These jails out here have plenty of room and with my luck I'll find out what those rooms look like pretty soon.* So I started thinking about how to get out of that mess.

That morning was it for me. I was done being "a bad guy." The next day I moved out and into the apartment of a friend of mine. A few days later, they all got busted in that old apartment. I had dodged a serious bullet.

The rest of that story isn't mine to tell. I just thought to myself, *That could be you, should have been you.* I got ready for class. I still had a future, and I was thankful for being called a drug dealer. It made me change. Hard work was more rewarding, and I slept much better.

By the way, soon after, another friend in Nebraska called me with a get-rich-quick scheme.

"I have a great idea. We need to get ourselves an old police dog."

"Police dog?" I asked him. "What are you talking about?"

"Listen," he said. "All those hotels on the highway—we know a lot of those dealers keep drugs in the car when they come to town. We take the dog out there to check all the cars and then we steal the drugs out of the car. The dealers can't call the police because how the fuck can they report stolen drugs?"

I said to him, "You're exactly right. They will not call the police. But they are going to try and find out who stole their drugs and the second you try and flip that stuff, they will hear about it and shoot you dead in the head."

Dumb fuck. I was so done with drugs.

CHAPTER 13

𝕭𝖆𝖈𝖐 𝖙𝖔 𝕮𝖆𝖑𝖎

𝕵 was still in school in Nebraska when my mom told me that Craig had been cheating on her. Again. She had found a bunch of evidence and when it finally blew up on him, he wanted to kick her out of the house, take the boats and the cars and everything my mom had worked so hard for. She played me the messages that he had left her and I got very upset. "Where is he now?" I asked. She told me he was going to watch my brother play baseball. So I drove over to the game and found Craig sitting in the bleachers.

I sat down next to him and right away he looked very nervous. "Craig, you know how much my mother means to me, right?" He nodded silently. "And you know that when it comes to my mom, there's nothing I wouldn't do to hurt someone if that someone tried to hurt her or steal from her, right?" He kept nodding. "And you know that I would gladly spend the next ten years of my life in a penitentiary for protecting my mother, right? And if I got out, and it was still happening, I would happily go back in the penitentiary to protect my mother. Do you understand where I'm coming from? Do you grasp this? Do we have a problem here or can we handle this with dignity and respect?"

He said quietly, "I think we can handle this the way you want to."

"Okay, good," I said. "You take your car, she keeps the house, and you can start your new life and be happy. That's what you can do, okay?"

And he said, "That's completely fair."

I went home and told my mom that everything was taken care of, but the minute I finished telling her, I realized it's not what she wanted to hear. She wanted to hear that he was going to come back to her, but I explained that was simply not in the cards. He had moved on and probably had a long time ago. She was heartbroken. No matter what he did, she cared for him. But, personally, I was glad to finally see it all end.

I went back out to Nebraska and resumed my life making pizzas (I had gotten a job at Pizza Hut) and cramming for the upcoming finals. A teammate came in to my dorm room one night and said, "Hey listen, there's an all-star football game being played out in Hawaii. I think you should go. Scouts are going to be there from all over the place—the Arena Football League, the NFL, Canadian Football League. The game is happening at the same time as the NFL Pro Bowl so all the right people will be out there on the island."

Well, that's all I had to hear. I headed off.

I played in this all-star game with a bunch of other college guys and NFL also-rans. It was obviously not the level I wanted to be at, but hey, it was better than making pizzas back in Nebraska. Thankfully, the guy throwing the event was a hot-shit agent, so he managed to have a lot of teams there taking looks at us. I was offered a contract by the Tri-City

Diesel of the Arena Football League. The trip had been worth it. Yes, I would be going back to Nebraska, but I would be going back with dignity. As a football player.

The season started that summer with practice sessions, and we had a decent season that first year. I made some really good friends and I managed to stay out of trouble. At one of our last games, I was setting up for a play inside the five-yard line and I looked up and saw my old girlfriend Amber staring at me from the stands. It had been very awkward when we had broken up, but there was still something about her. I saw her winking at me and I winked back; that's what we had done back when I was playing college ball. Feeling energized, knowing she was there, the next play I helped drive our guy into the end zone and we scored. After the game she came down to the field where I was signing autographs and we had a little talk. She told me she was engaged and was to be married. She wanted to see me, she said, one last time to know if what we had was real. I wasn't sure what was going on there. I told her to hang on; I went inside, showered, and came out and picked her up. We went back to my house to talk a little more.

I thought for sure something was in the cards for us that night. I thought she was coming back for one more special night together. But I was wrong. She literally had just wanted to see me to get some closure. That was the last time I saw Amber.

One of my teammates, Martin Fitzsimmons, rest in peace, was one of the coolest guys I knew back in the early 2000s. He and I formed a bond and, after the season when he went back down to Texas to train in his hometown, he took me with him. I just fell in love with his family. His dad was really old-school, and his mom was tough as nails. But I liked the structure and I liked the love in the household. They treated me like I belonged and made me wish I had been raised in that kind of house. Someone they knew died while I was down there and so that brought me to my first funeral. When I watched the family mourning, I realized I didn't know people well enough to cry like that. That made me sad. At that point, being in my early twenties, I think I was still very confused. I had never really had much structure, at least from a family standpoint, and whenever I got to see a family that really loved each other and respected each other, it made me realize what I was missing. I couldn't change my past, but I could certainly change my future if and when I started a family of my own. The Fitzsimmonses were good role models, and I made lots of mental notes while I was with them in the hopes that one day, I'd be a decent parent and a good family man like the examples that were being set in that household.

When I got back to Nebraska, I connected with an agent. He got me some tryouts and workout sessions to see about getting me to the next level. The Toronto Argonauts, the Buffalo Bills—I even had a workout with the Cowboys. During one of the drills, another player threw a cheap shot at me and it felt like he cracked a couple of my ribs. I was pissed off. For a few days it really hurt. I was sweating a lot; I just felt like it was going to kill me, but then the pain would pass so I didn't get it checked out. My agent told me that a team down in South Carolina, the Charleston Swamp Foxes, wanted me to fly down there so they could take a look at me. They were ready to offer me a deal, so they booked my flight and I made my way south. During the workouts that same pain by my ribs flared up—only twenty times worse. It was horrible, the worst pain I'd ever felt in my life, so they rushed me to the emergency room.

They couldn't figure out what was going on and then, wouldn't you know, this old Black female janitor was watching us in the emergency room and she said, "Hey baby, stand on one foot." I couldn't do it. She said simply, "It's his appendix." The nurses were like, *What?* So they made me drink this nasty-ass blue-dyed drink and, sure enough, that lady had been right. She may have saved my life. My appendix had exploded and an infection was spreading everywhere throughout my body. The doctor told me that I was a big guy and so this was going to be a tough surgery because they had to cut through "a lot of stuff." But it was like poison seeping through my system, so they had to get in there quick and clean everything up. While I was in the hospital after the operation, I also contracted pneumonia—which also almost killed me. I was very depressed. I had an opportunity with a new football team and other teams that had been interested in me; it was all going down the drain. The doctor said I was looking at three to four months of rehab and I said, "Look, I just got signed by the Charleston Swamp Foxes. I have to play football." The doctor said that wasn't going to happen. For the first three weeks in the hospital as my depression got deeper, all of those Black nurses made me get my ass out of bed. They took such good care of me, and they pushed me and made me walk around and get out of my funk.

The team basically said, "Let's wait a few months and see how you are and we'll take another look." But I did not want this opportunity to pass me by. I didn't know if it would ever happen again. So after about a month, I was back on the field against my doctor's orders trying to show them what I could do. I didn't have any feeling in my left leg, and I found it very hard to catch my breath at one point. My leg gave out on the field and I thought I'd torn my ACL. I could hear the coach saying, "Look, this guy is washed up." But I was not going to give up. I spent several weeks in rehab and, little by little, I started getting my swagger back. I did not want the ship to sail away without me. But it was all too little, too late. They didn't really want me anymore. But I did catch one final break. I got a call about playing back in California. A local semipro was going to pay me 1,500 bucks to play in a free-agent all-star game, and they moved me into a house in Pasadena. I got a job working part-time at a group home helping out troubled teens and I really liked that. I played in that all-star game at the Staples Center and had one of the best games of my football career. I had three sacks, a "scoop-and-score" fumble recovery—just a very strong game and I felt great. At one point, I was chasing the quarterback in the second half, and my leg went numb again. I fell to the ground and I couldn't get up. I thought I pulled a hamstring. I limped off the field and didn't finish the game. I knew I was done with football. That part of my life was over.

Working at a group home seemed like my destiny now. *I'll just teach kids*, I thought. By now I had graduated from college with a BS in education with an emphasis in special needs, and my degree was soon put to good use when I started working as a recreation therapist at a place called Five Acres in Altadena, California. As they describe their organization, "Since our beginnings as an orphanage in downtown Los Angeles, Five Acres has been committed to strengthening children and families and empowering them within their communities. Now as one of the county's oldest nonprofits, today we strive for permanency: a permanent, loving family for every child in our care. We offer a full continuum of care for children and families in crisis, including foster care, adoption, deaf services, therapeutic residential care for foster youth and community-based mental/behavioral health programs."

In addition to working as a therapist there, I would also substitute teach when I was needed (they had a school within the facility). I always got along great with kids, and there I was being given opportunities for me to make a positive difference in their lives. Usually, I worked with seven-to-nine-year-old boys and girls and, sometimes, even younger kids—in the three-to-six-year age range.

Dealing with this group of children, the "forgotten ones," could be tough. We are talking about crack babies with parents in jail, kids abused and destroyed at five years old. It was my job to teach them how to have fun again, build hand-to-eye coordination, and more. Those children became easily frustrated, so it was my job to help them build little successes. I'm not really sure why I was good at this. I mean, yes, I went to school for it, but there was a lot more to it than what was in books. You just had to have a feel for those kids. You had to be able to relate to them because otherwise, no trust could be built. I tried to teach those kids everything I could, but in reality, I think they were teaching me just as much about myself. You see, they made me realize that I was equipped for the job because at one time I had been very much like them. They helped me understand my own childhood and make sense of it. I learned through those experiences that, as a teacher, you always have to be open to learning more. You can never assume that you have all of the answers.

CHAPTER 14

𝕷𝖆𝖗𝖗𝖞 𝕻𝖔𝖑𝖑𝖆𝖈𝖐

𝕴 had been making about 1,500 bucks per game playing football and I was also working in the group home when I started bouncing at clubs. I got the gig through some of the other guys on the team who had already been working for a guy named Larry Pollack. He was a very successful club owner in Los Angeles. Keys, his biggest bodyguard, was a guy who worked for Larry at night and spent his days heading up the bodyguard team for Snoop Dogg. He was one of the first guys I met at the club. Keys was a story in himself. Six feet tall and a biscuit away from five hundred pounds. Broad shoulders, mahogany dark, and as big and bad as it got. Except for one thing. I say this with all the love in the world because Keys would soon become an important part of my existence...but dude had a voice like Mickey Mouse. Like, what the actual fuck? Biggest badass motherfucker, and that voice? Made no sense. But it didn't matter. Keys was Keys and there was nobody else like him.

But back to Larry. He had created a chain called the Saddle Ranch Chop House that had a number of locations in the western United States, but the main place was located at Universal City. It was an absolute zoo. Any Friday night you might have more than two thousand people in the place. They came from all over—from the high desert, from the beach, from Orange County. It was a magnet for young people who wanted to dance, eat good food, and, of course, drink lots and try to hook up with somebody. The drinks were big, the food was over-the-top, and there was always a good number of really good-looking women there. Larry's laid-back look (he was always wearing stylish jeans and flip-flops) totally belied how crazy the place was. He was cocky, and he was somewhat arrogant, but, to me, the dude had earned it. He had built a successful business which totally played into the visceral desires of the young and hungry. Smart business plan. What I got to know about him I liked. He ran a good business. He was a stickler for excellence and I'm always down with that. If a waitress didn't know the menu by heart, she was fired, no questions asked. If the bartender over-served so much as one customer, done. There was no middle ground. If you worked for Larry, you operated at a high level or you didn't operate at all. My friend that got me in there explained to me that there were two security teams, one on the inside and one at the door. He also told me that they were like oil and water. It was a very competitive scene among the bouncers, and each team wanted to make the other one look as shitty as possible. I was down with that. It was just like in sports. If you're not out there trying to show the other guy up, maybe you shouldn't be on the field. Sure, we were working for the same team, but it was still competitive. Game on, bitches.

I was placed with the team that worked the door. Now, this was a scene. People would do just about anything to get into that club. We were the frontline, and so naturally club-goers would try to win us over; grease us with whatever it took. We were each getting paid about 250 bucks per night, salary. But that was nothing compared to the little racket that was going on when I got there. Guys would take money to let people cut the line, to let them in if they forgot their IDs, and stuff like that. At the end of the night, you might be looking at an additional $2,000–$3,000. Paychecks didn't matter. Oftentimes, we would forget to even pick those up because they paled so much in comparison to what we were hustling off the books upfront.

I had a lot going on at that time. I was bouncing and working at the group home and playing football and getting my life together. I had a car, I was paying my bills, and I was making a fortune at the Saddle Ranch Chop House. All of us bouncers were becoming almost like local celebrities. We were part of the show. We were big, we were funny, and we were in charge of the night. You did not get in if we did not want you to get in. There was one guy in the crew, though, who didn't take part in our little racket. His name was Rico, and he was a real law-and-order guy. He wasn't a big guy at all, but I knew he was strong. It just annoyed the crap out of me and the other guys that he was keeping such a tight eye on us. And then he did it. He ratted all of us out to the manager. Looking back, I can't say I blame him. And I'm sure Larry appreciated the fact that he had somebody minding the store. But it still sucked. Larry fired all of us. Somehow or another, though, I got to stay on. But not in the same capacity. From that point on, I was to work with the inside crew. There would be no other opportunities to shake people down at the door. That was probably a good thing for me. I needed to work, and I knew all along what

I was doing was wrong, despite the animosity and tension that had existed between the two groups of bodyguards. Once I got to know the inside team, I really liked them a lot. Just a great squad of guys. I made lifelong friends with most of them, including a guy named Big Tiny, who was seven feet tall. He and I could pass for brothers. There was also Big Phil, Beau the Rapper, Big Mike (who at one time had played for the Atlanta Hawks), and several others. However, I was surprised to see that Rico was now also part of this team. Was he placed there to keep an eye on me? I had no idea, but I wasn't too happy about it.

We didn't wear headsets on the floor. Most of us were big enough that we could see over everybody and we communicated with hand gestures and eye contact. Eventually, most of us would end up taking road trips with Larry when he visited other clubs around the country, but for the most part, I was stationed at Universal City. What's more, Rico and I became partners, kind of like two cops riding in the same vehicle. I still had somewhat of an attitude toward him, but he really won me over one night. A fight broke out and he and I raced over and put one of the guys in a chokehold and blacked him out in just a few seconds. I was impressed. Also, our size differences made us an effective team. The fact that I was so big distracted people, and that allowed Rico to put them down on the ground when he needed to.

Rico was basically Larry's right-hand man and I know a lot of the other bodyguards held that against him. But you know what? It wasn't a bad role to have. Most of us were probably a little bit jealous. Then, little by little, Rico and I start becoming tight. We discovered we were both big WrestleMania fans and we really bonded over that. He would try to bust me on WrestleMania trivia and I was like, *Are you kidding me, bro?* Rico was a cool dude. I forgave him for ratting us out because, honestly, he was just doing his job. That was a learning moment for me.

I was working about four nights a week at the Saddle Ranch Chop House and I was really settling in with my life. I had started dating a girl and we moved in together. Things were becoming stable. I was paying my bills, I had a nice little life at home, I was working my ass off, and I was starting to feel like a responsible human being. But, of course, this was *my* life, which meant that nothing could remain stable for long. I went to Las Vegas as part of Larry's traveling security team for a few days and, when I got back to my house, there was a red lock on my door. There was also a sign taped to the window from the sheriff's department. I had been evicted. I peeked in the windows and saw that all the furniture was gone. I broke into the place and saw that my girlfriend had gathered up everything of value and left. I had trusted her to kind of run the household. She was paying the bills, supposedly, and all that sort of stuff. But in reality, she had not done any of that. She let everything go into default and then just up and left. I tried calling her but her phone number no longer worked. She had also taken all the money out of our account and left me high and dry. So there I was, ready to restart the couch-surfing cycle.

The story of my fucking life.

CHAPTER 15

Snoop

Everything had basically dissolved before my eyes. On top of my girlfriend screwing me over by running off with everything and getting me evicted, I was also about to leave my job at the group home over a situation that arose after a series of events that I can't go into here, but really became impossible to navigate. I did nothing wrong. In fact. I think I did everything *right*, but sometimes the powers that be can't handle too much "right." Bottom line, it was time to move on. Plus, I knew that teaching kids was in my future and that I'd always want to keep doing that.

The only thing that was really going well for me was body-guarding at the Saddle Ranch. It was, in its own crazy and chaotic way, a reliable gig. I mean, no two nights were ever the same, and things got out of control frequently, but at least I knew what I was getting into each night and the money was solid even though we weren't taking cuts at the front door. Interestingly, it was my burgeoning friendship with Rico that really helped me stay focused and on some kind of track. I had been putting on a lot of weight. Working in that club, most of us ate like wild animals, and I can't remember a meal that didn't end with a giant apple cobbler right out of the oven with a scoop of vanilla ice cream on top the size of a softball. I was getting big. One day at work, Rico pulled me aside and he said, "Dude, there's something different about you. You're a smart guy, you're a funny guy, and you have a lot of charisma. I think there's a lot you're going to do in this life, but you are eating yourself to death right now. I train over at Gold's Gym. Why don't you start coming with me and get yourself in shape? You're throwing your life away right now. You could actually be in the WWE if you took care of yourself and I'm telling you, I'll work with you and I'll train with you and get you already. I believe in you."

Sometimes there are people in life that probably have no idea the difference they make in your future. I think back to that little speech Rico made to me, and without it, I'm not sure you would even be holding a book in your hands right now. And he just kept at it. "I know your girl dumped you, I know you're embarrassed and humiliated right now. She burned you. So get *pissed*! Use that in the gym! Make it stoke your fire!"

By that time, I had also reached out to Larry to ask him for a loan so that I could get my own place to live, and he obliged. Wasn't what I really wanted to do; I mean, when a rich guy loans you money, there's no way you'll ever get out of paying it back on time, but it was cool. He helped me out, deducted it from my pay, but it was all good. Saved my ass, in fact.

I started going to Gold's Gym with Rico and he and a trainer there really kicked my ass. But it was awesome. Little by little, I started to get in shape and watch what I was eating. Rico stayed on me, always drilling into me that he believed in me.

He didn't want to see me fuck up whatever might be out there on the horizon for me. By this time, I was getting concerned about my future because football had become a distant speck in the rearview mirror ever since that 2005 free-agent all-star game at Staples Center. That dream was done. But listening to Rico, the seeds of new dreams were being planted in my psyche. He was giving me hope.

One fateful night at the club, a huge fight broke out with a bunch of gang members. It was ugly. I got right in middle of it to start pulling guys apart and throwing them out. I turned the wrong way at one point, however, and took a pretty good punch on my cheek. It was hard enough that I was bleeding heavily inside my mouth and I could feel a piece of skin hanging off in there. It hurt pretty bad, which made me really angry. I grabbed the guy who hit me as he tried to run away, and, let's just say he is probably still bruised to this day.

The rapper Petey Pablo was in the house that night. He shared a manager with Snoop Dogg and, all of a sudden, I got word that Snoop's team thought I might be a good fit to help look after him after a few of his guys saw me in action that night "cleaning house."

I'll be up front. I'm an Ice Cube guy. I love Ice Cube. So when I got the offer to bodyguard for Snoop, that's what I was thinking. *Snoop's okay, but he's no Ice Cube.* Well, how soon my attitude became adjusted! Snoop, as I would soon learn, was the greatest. What can you say about this dude? He's an international icon, famous all over the world, and loved by many. Calvin Broadus, AKA Snoop Dogg, first burst on the scene back in 1992 when he was featured in Dr. Dre's debut single, "Deep Cover," and then on Dre's debut solo album, *The Chronic*. A year after that came Snoop's debut solo album, *Doggystyle*, produced by Dr. Dre and released by Death Row records. It debuted at number one on the popular albums chart, selling almost one million copies in its first week. He was an instant star. The dude has sold more than thirty-five million albums all over the world. He's more than just a rapper today. He's a singer, actor, record producer, businessman, and football coach. There is nobody else like Snoop Dogg in the world.

Still, you don't bodyguard as a fan. You put all of your personal feelings aside and you just do the job. Snoop was my first actual "celebrity" client. I had bodyguarded for lots of rich people, but celebrities have different concerns. Another thing is, when you're a bodyguard for a celebrity, you often become a celebrity yourself because the cameras always capture you standing next to the celebrity. That's where some bodyguards get themselves in trouble. They begin to think that they are a celebrity because all of a sudden, they're getting lots of attention. That's a trap that you can never fall into. Thankfully, I never had that problem. I watched it happen to a lot of other guys. A woman could cause you to not do your job, and then you'd be out of a job. If she suckers you in so that you're not paying attention to your client—and then maybe a friend of hers sneaks through and gets to your client to hassle him or do whatever—it's not good. Fame by osmosis, it's dangerous. Me, as a bodyguard I never minded being the bad guy. In fact, it just goes with the job. Your entire purpose is to crush dreams. I know that sounds harsh, but you have to adopt that attitude or you might let your guard down. People come at you with a million different excuses and reasons to let them in. But you just can't do it. My attitude has always been focus on me; focus your hatred on me, then you're leaving my client alone.

It was Keys from the Saddle Ranch Chop House who was the connection to Snoop; he worked for him, too. We'd had some friction over the years, but overall, he was a stand-up guy and I respected him. He explained to me that my first assignment working for Snoop would be an overnight shift where I would just sit outside his house. Pretty basic. Keys said to me, "You just sit here and see if he comes outside the house. Just watch the driveway. If he comes out and gets in his car, you follow him wherever he goes. Never let him out of your sight. And most importantly, do not fall asleep."

That would, of course, be the worst thing you could do. You can never fall asleep when you're on an overnight, but it's tough. By three or four a.m., you're bored out of your mind, but it doesn't matter. There was another car there with another guy in it—the guy who rolled Snoop's joints. He would be watching the house as well. It was the two of us on duty. I made it through the night okay, but by five a.m., I was blinking pretty hard, trying to stay awake. Then I noticed what I thought was a woman walking out of the front door across the driveway. This person was wearing a silk robe and their hair was all tied up in a wrap. I did a double take and realized it was Snoop himself. I got out of my car just to make a quick introduction and I noticed the other bodyguard had fallen asleep in his car. On my way over to see Snoop I tried to wake the guy up by tapping on the windows, but it was no use. This motherfucker was out deep—in serious REM land. The windows were fogged up from his snoring. "It's cool," Snoop said. "Let him sleep, no big deal." Hey, as long as Snoop wasn't upset, I was not going to question my boss. We said a quick hello, and then Snoop popped into his pimped-out, black Pittsburgh Steeler truck. I jumped back in my car and followed him. In a few minutes we pulled up in front of Denny's. Snoop got out of his truck and came over to me with a hundred-dollar bill and said, "Can you go inside and pick up my order?" "No problem," I said. What was funny was the order actually came to $106 so I covered the rest myself. I must have proven myself because I got home later that morning and Keys called me and said, "Okay, you're good. I want you working there on Monday and Tuesday nights." And that was it. So I just factored that into my schedule. By that time, I had lost about sixty-five pounds going to the gym with Rico, I was working at the Saddle Ranch Chop House, and I was also helping to protect one of the biggest names in entertainment. Things finally seemed like they might be coming together a little bit.

Snoop was doing a big show in Anaheim at the Pond Arena. He needed some help on his crew because that night after the show, everybody was hopping on a plane, heading over to Europe for a tour. Since the full-time bodyguards who were traveling with him would be home packing, I got the call to help out at the arena. I met Snoop and his crew in the parking lot and we headed toward the backstage area. I was the only guy who didn't have a backstage laminate and one of the arena guards stopped me and said, "Where's your badge?" "Body-guards don't need badges," I said to him gruffly and pushed through. Shortly after I was positioned out in front of Snoop's dressing room when this large Black guy tried to walk past me and through the door. I stepped in his way.

"What do you think you're doing?" he said.

"I don't know who you are, so I can't let you through."

"I'm your boss, motherfucker."

"Really? What's my boss's name?"

"Big Papa."

Shit. I had heard about Big Papa. He *was* my boss. "My bad," I said. But his eyes lit up. "No, no, it's cool, good job," he said.

At that moment the backstage door opened up and Snoop poked his head out. "What's going on?" I heard him say. He had heard our little ruckus.

"All is cool," Big Papa said. "I like this guy," he added, motioning to me.

This was good. Some other people tried to work their way back to the dressing room and I shut them all down instantly. And I was pretty rough with a couple of them. "Mean mugging" is what it came to be called when I gave these guys the "no you don't" look. One guy started saying, "Snoop is expecting me," and I said, "You know what, if he was expecting you, I would have known about it. So fuck you."

"Big Papa," I said that first time I met him, "I'm going to say no. Whoever comes up to the door, the answer is no. That's what I'm paid to do." Big Papa seemed even more impressed.

I got to watch a little bit of the show once Snoop went on and it was very impressive. After the show, we were all getting ready to leave and go back out to the cars and Big Papa says, "Come out to the airport with us. If you don't mind, continue your shift until we take off tonight." That was no problem. We drove out to nearby John Wayne Airport; the bodyguards that were making the trip showed up and I helped see the party off. The next morning, I got a call from Snoop's office asking me about a passport because they wanted me to hop a plane and make my way to London. But I couldn't go because I was already booked on some other jobs. As it turns out, I'm glad I didn't go because once they arrived in Europe there were lots of problems with his giant entourage and some arrests were made when some of his people were not allowed into the

Admiral's Club at the airport. But once they got back, I was back out there with Snoop.

I resumed going out to his house for driveway detail and then also got to go inside his house a few times to stand guard. As much as I love telling stories and telling jokes, that wasn't part of my gig was there. That wasn't what I was getting paid to do with them. That said, Snoop could also be very chatty and sometimes in the limousine, walking to a club door or even in his own driveway, he would start a conversation with me. He would ask my opinion about certain things. And I was happy to answer him. But only because he had initiated the conversation. That's nothing I ever would be doing my own and, to be honest, when he would do that, it made me focus even more on what was going on around him. Because I knew I was being a little bit distracted. I only spoke when I was spoken to.

I liked Snoop. He treated me with respect and I gave him my best. To be a good bodyguard, you have to believe in yourself. You can't worry about getting approval. And you never want to get comfortable on the job. That's why you don't try to become friends. You can respect your boss, and you can admire the work that they do, but the minute you sit down and start watching TV with them, then someone is not watching the door. The second you get caught up in the lights and the glamour, that's when someone's going to make a move. None of this shit has anything to do with you. If it's a celebrity client, they have earned their place in the spotlight. You have not. So just because you're lucky enough to be in there sometimes, don't start thinking for a second you have earned it. Because you haven't. If you're true to your instincts and you genuinely take care of your client, the friendship will happen once you stop working for them. That's a different story. I love my friendship with Snoop today because I know it's based on a foundation where I always had his back no matter what. He knew that, and he appreciated that.

Something I noticed about Snoop almost instantly was how much good work he did for other people. Coming out of Long Beach, he was truly a local icon and he did a lot for those neighborhoods where he came from. If somebody's mom died, he would pay for the funeral. Somebody needed help starting a business, he was right there to help out. Of course, all of those things led to even more people wanting to get close to him, so it made my job tougher. Still, that's who he was and what he did, and I had to deal with that. It blew my mind how much he did for people. He started local youth football leagues and paid for everything. He was a genuinely good person who understood the power of his celebrity. People freaked out when they saw Snoop. They couldn't believe it was him in person. And again, I had to be the bad guy and keep those people away.

Working as a bodyguard for Snoop really taught me the art of looking for things before they happened. Shutting down the things early. That was always the key. Not to wait until it got out of control. If you saw somebody you thought was going to hassle Snoop, you didn't wait to act. You needed to defuse the situation early. Snoop's celebrity was so huge that he did attract many kinds of fanatics, and so my radar got really good at detecting who was going to make a run at my client. When I would shut people down, often incorporating funny little one-liners, Snoop would chuckle. Sometimes he would mutter out of the side of his mouth to me, "What the fuck did you just say?" And I would just smile and say, "Keep moving, boss. Keep moving. Let's get you out of here in one piece."

I worked closely with Snoop's manager, Kevin, an awesome guy who may just be the whitest guy on the planet. He's a Canadian, and he and I had one of the greatest working relationships of anyone I have ever bodyguarded for. Kevin is just a straight-shooting, logical, hard-working guy who dedicates his life to his clients, especially Snoop. And it can be frustrating. A lot of Kevin's job was just making sure that Snoop showed up on time for things, and I knew that Snoop ran on the late side. We would start working out things where we would tell Snoop he had be somewhere at ten even though it wasn't until eleven. If the plane was leaving at noon, we told Snoop it was leaving at ten. Just to make sure.

One time, Snoop wanted to go to the Staples Center to watch the Lakers play. He's a big Laker fan. He was bringing his whole family to the game, and when he had his family with him, he really did not want to be bothered. Family time for Snoop was always sacred. I'm a Celtics guy and, that night, the Lakers were playing the Celtics. I knew I was going to see Kevin Garnett, Rondo, and the rest—in the flesh—and I was jazzed. When I met Snoop at his house to leave for the game his wife said about me, "What's with this guy in the Celtics jacket?" "I told you about this guy," Snoop chuckled. "This guy thinks for himself."

When we got the Staples Center, Ice Cube was sitting courtside right by where Snoop would be. Cube, like Snoop, is a huge Lakers guy. "You let this motherfucker in with a Celtics jacket?" Cube said to Snoop. Snoop opened his eyes wide and said, "You see the size of this dude? Do you want to tell him to take it off?" Everybody laughed at that. And everybody in the crowd wanted a piece of Snoop that night. There's no hiding when you're sitting courtside, and I knew it was going to be crazy. But when everybody wants a piece of your client, I'm the storm in your summer day. I'm going to ruin it for you. I was shutting people down with one-liners and Snoop kept telling his wife and Cube, laughing, "I told you this guy is cool. And he's pretty funny, too." Sylvester Stallone jumped out of nowhere to say hi to Snoop and I was thinking, *Dude, this is really Sylvester Stallone?* He'd had a little bit of work done. This was not Rocky we are talking about. Something was happening to this guy. But this was life in Hollywood. You never knew what celebrities may jump out and want to say hi. Snoop is a magnet not for just people in the street, but for some of the most famous people on the planet.

Once Snoop was settled in courtside, Kevin and I were given a couple tickets to watch the game from upstairs, which was a really nice perk because I had not expected that. Normally I would be waiting underneath the stands for that text from Snoop telling me he was ready to leave. But on that night, I got a treat.

After a few months working with Snoop I came to realize that he is a very special kind of celebrity. He takes nothing for granted, he works really hard, and he's all about giving back. Most people will never hear about half the shit that Snoop does. He just does it.

CHAPTER 16

The WWE Calls

One night, a group of WWE guys showed up at the club. I have to admit I was kind of excited to see a few wrestlers pulling up to the front. I knew right then and there I would make sure that I got them VIP access and placement in the club. I was still a wrestling guy, even though I had a horrible meeting up in Toronto. The wrestlers came in with a guy named Tommy Dreamer. He was the executive vice president of talent relations for WWE. I knew who he was. He was a big shot, and he was a totally cool guy. Once I got all the guys settled at the VIP table, Tony kept coming over to me to say thank you. He seemed like a quality dude and, I have to admit, I appreciated the fact that I was getting some attention from a guy of his stature.

At one point during the night, I could see a guy on the dance floor making some trouble. At least I assumed some guy was making trouble because I saw a girl disappear down into the crowd, like Jaws had gotten her by the legs and yanked her down. I'm six-foot-eight and I was looking across the room, over the tops of all the patron's heads, at other guys who worked there, and we were all making eye contact. We knew what we had to do. We all had to get over there and get over there fast. I got to the middle of the dance floor and I found the girl on the floor and pulled her up. I wanted this one. I watched it happen and I wanted to make sure she was okay.

"Are you okay?" I asked her.

"I'm cool," she said, "but these two guys have really been hassling me. They kept grabbing my ass and then they pulled me down to the floor." She motioned to who did it and it was actually two midgets. I was like, *What?* She didn't want any more hassles; she was willing to let it go, but I said to the two guys, "Both of you back off or I'm going to throw you out." Well, with that, one of the midgets stepped up and boom! punched me right in the stomach. It didn't do much, I was okay, and I said to him in surprise, "Dude, you just hit me?" "Yeah," he said confidently, as if he was going to do it again. I grabbed him to throw him out and then, wouldn't you know it, the other midget hit me as well. Well, this was going to be easy. I picked up both of them, one in each hand, in a little move I like to call "the suitcase." I literally just had them by the belt buckles and carried them out the front door. I dumped them on the street and told them to get the hell out and not come back.

Some of the other guys by the door were cracking up and as I turned to go back inside, I bumped into Tommy Dreamer, who had watched the whole scene and followed me out. "That was the most amazing shit I have ever seen! What do you call that move?" I told him it was "the suitcase" and he laughed his ass off. "Listen," he said, "I'm the head of talent relations for WWE. I think we might be able to work together." My mind flashed back to the meeting up in Toronto. I told him a little bit about it and he brushed it off. "Don't worry about that. Come in for a workout and then let's talk, okay?"

This was my chance. But I had to let Snoop know. I called Keys and let him know to take me off the schedule. I saw Snoop once more and I said, "Boss, I'm not even sure if this is the right thing to do, but it's something I've always dreamed of."

Snoop said, "Are you kidding? You have to do this. You know how much I love wrestling. I want to see you wrestle one day. You can always come back. If something doesn't work out, you can always work for me. I like you and I trust you, but most importantly, my family likes and trust you. That goes a long way with me. But go become a wrestler. That's what you need to do. That's your dream."

With Snoop's and Keys's blessings, I made the decision to do it.

CHAPTER 17

McDonough, Georgia

Three months went by after meeting Tommy that night, and then I got a call from John Laurinaitis. A famed former pro wrestler himself, known as "Johnny Ace," he went on to become the head of talent relations for WWE.

He said to me in his deep, gravelly voice, "I saw your photo and I liked it. So we're bringing you down to McDonough, Georgia, to see what you've got."

This was getting exciting. I took two weeks off and hit the road for Georgia. Once I got down there, I met Bill DeMott, another former wrestler, but he had turned into a WWE trainer. I was a fan and I liked him.

Once I got settled into my dorm room, they started putting me through some drills. It was tough work. My goal during all of the drills was the same one I had when I was a football player: just don't finish last. But it was a shitload of work. After a couple of grueling days, Bill looked me up and down and said, "So what do you call yourself?"

"Just George," I said.

He laughed. "Okay, look, for right now I'm just going to call you 'King Biscuit.' You're the biggest guy here. So that's your name for now. We will start with that, and we'll see where it goes."

Then it was back to the drills. The footwork was confusing, but little by little I got used to it. They taught me how to hit the ropes. They taught me all about crossovers. They taught me how to go down without getting hurt. It really was boot camp. At night, I would fill my bathtub with ice cubes and look at all the bruises across my back in the mirror. Bill was really trying to break me down, but that was okay. I knew what he was doing. He was trying to get to the bottom of what I was. He wanted to see what I was made of. The bottom line was, he was trying to see if I was a wrestler in my heart.

A lot of guys come in imagining the glory and the success. They envision what it's like to be a celebrity wrestler. But that doesn't mean it's in their hearts. Bill wanted somebody who was willing to make a career out of wrestling and be able to absorb whatever the sport threw at you. He was trying to separate the men from the boys, and, in the process, he was helping me turn into a man. There were other wrestlers down there, too, and I could tell not all of them wanted it as badly as I did. I just kept my nose to the grindstone and did whatever he told me to do in that ring, and then a little bit more.

It took me a while, and there were definitely nights when I wondered if I had what it took. Football had been tough, but this was ridiculous. It was hotter than hell down in McDonough. There was no air conditioning anywhere and they worked us like dogs. On certain nights I would lay in bed looking at the ceiling, thinking to myself, *Am I kidding myself? Do I really want this? I've got a good life back in California. Do I want to give it up for this shot?* And over time, the more I asked myself those questions, the more the answer in my head became *Yes, I want to do this. Yes, I believe I can do this. Yes, I will do this.*

In addition to wrestling, of course, you've got to have personality. After all, the best wrestlers in the world are known for their personalities. And your personality comes out when they put a video camera on you and you start doing promos. Just as important as the drills in the ring was how you did when that camera was pointed at you. I felt like I had a natural gift for performance, and many of those around me in McDonough seemed to agree. My promos at the beginning were not great, but they weren't bad either. I would get a little nervous and I would get scared, but little by little I developed a reputation. And the camera seemed to like me. Then it was back in the ring for endless crisscross drills with other wrestlers, when the powers that be really tried to break you down. The training would take inexperienced guys and put them through the pain. To give them tastes of what it really felt like. And it only got tougher.

I impressed everybody that was watching with every drill they threw at me. As the days went on, Bill kept saying to me, "There's something about you. There's really something about you that I like. You've got something, kid. I can't quite put my finger on it, but I'm liking it." At the end of the few weeks down there, Johnny pulled me aside and said, "Okay, look. Lose fifty pounds and I'll give you a contract, okay? Can you do that? It's not as much as you think. You can do it. It's only fifty pounds." I told him he could count on me, and then I drove back to California. I called my buddy Rico and he and I started hitting the gym every day. In two months, I lost a hundred pounds and I was in the best shape of my life. I was feeling great. I could do it.

Right around that time, *SmackDown* was coming to Los Angeles and Johnny arranged an invite for me. I showed up that night, went backstage, and I was in awe. I walked in the building and the first guy I saw was Cowboy Bob Ward, one of the greatest workers in our business. He looked at me and said, "You've got a good look, kid." Coming from him, that meant the world. Had I really just stepped into this situation? The kid who loved wrestling now had a chance of actually being a WWE wrestler? *Pinch me. Just fucking pinch me.*

Around the corner came the one and only Rowdy Roddy Piper. He asked me if I needed anything. *Say what?* Damn, I was like a pig in shit. I could not grasp the reality of that. Trevor Murdoch came over and introduced himself and I said to him, "That's my last name, too!" He laughed and said "That's not my real last name, bro. It's a gimmick." When Johnny saw me, he looked me up and down and said, "You look like a million bucks. Seriously, you look great, and I'll have your contract to you next week. Welcome aboard." I simply said, "Thanks, boss." And then I started thinking about moving to McDonough, Georgia. Before the night was over, though, there was one other person I was going to meet. Before the wrestling got underway, Johnny said, "I'd like to introduce you to Vince." Vince McMahon? The guy who built my childhood? I wasn't sure I was ready for that. I think Johnny could see it in my face. "Relax, kid. You're okay. You're one of us now. Act like it. Vince is a good guy. He needs to smell confidence on you. Are you ready?"

We turned the corner and there he was. It was like seeing a Mount Rushmore face come to life. He was bigger than I imagined. His face was chiseled, and his eyes were boring into me. It was all too brief. "Nice to meet you, sir," I said, extending my hand.

"You've got a good strong handshake," he said to me, squeezing right back as a show of his own strength. "It's good to have you aboard."

CHAPTER 18

WWE: 2006–2008

You always remember the first time you go through the curtain. Me, I was terrified. At least for the first few seconds. But that's how I was. Even when I was playing football, I would get butterflies on the kickoff. But after that first snap, it would all fall into place. "Comfortable sweat" is what I called it. Once that kicked in, I was fine. It was the same thing that started happening with wrestling. I would have those butterflies, and I would go out there, feel the crowd, and, no matter what else was going on, I would be okay. It was one thing to be wrestling in the Deep South in front of three hundred people in some little place buried in a shopping center. That wasn't the big time. The big time is when you get called up to go out on the road to perform in arenas. I had only been a Deep South wrestler for a few months when I got the call. There's nothing like getting that first call. "George, we want you out there. This is your moment." To someone that had worshipped wrestlers since he was a little kid but had never been able to afford to go watch an actual match—I mean, like a big match in a huge space—getting that call was a pretty big deal.

Tonight I would be working under my agent, the legendary Dean Malenko, "Man of a thousand holds." He was totally the real deal. He had been born into a wrestling family. His father, Boris, was a well-known wrestler. Dean started out working as a referee in Florida and eventually worked his way up to reffing WWF matches in the mid-1980s. He himself went on to wrestle all over the world in many different capacities and configurations. He retired from wrestling in the early 2000s, and by the time I had entered the sport, he was a very influential coach and agent.

One of my first reactions when I got the call to go on the road was that I didn't have anything cool to wear. A little-known fact is that wrestlers basically buy their own stuff. It comes right out of your own pocket. At that point, I looked like an escapee from Urban Outfitters. My look was terrible. Camo pants and these stupid-ass boots...I really had not taken a lot of time to get a "look" together because I didn't think this would be happening so soon. But there I was flying from Florida to Cleveland, where I would make my debut. I saw Montel Vontavious Porter (aka MVP) at the airport, and he told me he would ride with me to the arena. But the flight got delayed and I was really freaking out. I was going to be late for my big moment in the sun. We finally got to Cleveland and rented a car, but then we could not find the arena. It might have been funny had it not felt like the biggest chance of my life was going right down the toilet before my eyes. We finally got there and we were met by Dean who said to me, "You are up in fifteen minutes." It was Christmas week, the place was sold out and rocking, and I had not had any time to work anything out beforehand. Nevertheless, I got to my place, the curtain opened up, and I heard my music kick in:

"Diesel Fluid" from Wu-Tang Clan and Method Man. When you go through the curtain, it's almost like going through a pane of water. You feel something in front of you that you have penetrated. And then when you get out under the lights, you can't believe how warm it is. It's like a big hug, in a way. Now, people had no idea who I was and so they started booing me. But that was okay. I knew that's how it went, and I was cool with that. This was pro wrestling. You couldn't get hung up on having people hate you.

Scotty 2 Hotty was waiting for me when I climbed into the ring and he said to me, "Take your tank top off and throw it at me." That's how things would get started. Well, I did what he told me to do, and then I yelled "Wooh!" Now if you know anything about wrestling, you know that that exclamation is basically owned by Ric Flair. You can't be making that sound in any kind of wrestling match and expect to be taken seriously. But yeah, that's what came out of me. I regretted it instantly. But we still had a match to get through. He hit me with a couple of dropkicks and then I hit him with a pretty savage clothes-line. Back when I was in McDonough, trainer Bill DeMott worked with us on Japanese-style wrestling, which is very physical. In that training, he taught me the Burning Hammer; unfortunately, in this match, Scotty was not expecting such a monster hammer from a beast like me. It caught him off guard and I knew he wasn't happy. Like, he seemed seriously pissed off. We still got through the match; I picked him up, dropped him down, heard one-two-three get counted out, and I had won my first match. I was really happy. Sort of.

I tramped back to the locker room. I saw Dean; I saw the late, great Chris Benoit as well as Booker T—everybody was waiting back there. One of them said to me, "How do you think

119

you did?" Inside, I thought I had done okay, but I also knew I had fucked up by hitting him too hard. So I said, "I give myself C-minus." They all basically agreed with me. The report on me was not positive. A couple of nights later they sent me home. I was devastated. It was basically like I was being fired. It still had been thrilling getting my one shot in front of a full house like that. But I truly expected to be cut loose completely because I had not delivered the right performance.

Mike Bucci, director of talent, called me and I said to him, "You're going to fire me, right?" He said calmly, "No, George. We're actually giving you a little bit of a raise and shifting you up to developmental. We know your flight got delayed and you were stressed out. Scotty didn't want to work with you, and that happens. But we still think you've got something worth working on and so we're keeping you." To say I dodged a major bullet is an understatement.

In Georgia, a short while later, Bill DeMott called me into his office and said, "Guess what? Dusty Rhodes, the American Dream, is coming down today. I know how much he means to you, I know you look up to him, and I would like you to meet him." I couldn't believe it. What would I say to one of my wrestling heroes? I was so nervous.

When he walked in later that day, wearing a Texas Longhorn hat, a flannel shirt, and jeans, I didn't know what to say. I meekly stuck my hand out and said, "Mr. Rhodes, my name is George Murdoch." He gruffly blew me off, saying, "I only talk to stars, baby!" Wait a minute, what? That kind of pissed me off. I would learn later he was just fucking with me and that's how he was. But in that moment, deep inside, I thought to myself, *I will show you, Mr. Legend. I may be a big fan of yours, but I also believe in myself and I have every intention of making it as a wrestler.* My one thought then was, *It's true: don't meet your heroes because they will only let you down.* But I was too immature to realize what was going on. A few months later, I saw him again, this time in Florida after I moved down there. I walked into his dressing room where he was holding court. It was really warm. "You gonna rest your fat ass in front of the air conditioner?" he chuckled at me. "Hey, it's not my fault you picked the wrong seat," I shot back. Well, he laughed at that. We started talking some trash. I cracked him up a couple more times and, all of a sudden, he wasn't acting like such a big shot anymore. He actually seemed to like what I was dishing out.

I cut a promo a few nights after that and he stood there watching me, nodding. He came over to me afterward and said, "I can help mold you. I see a lot of me in you. I know what you're about, and I want to help you." I tried playing it cool, but inside I was squealing like a little kid. Little did I know that Dusty Rhodes, the American Dream, was about to become my mentor and someone I trusted more than anybody else in wrestling. He was like a father figure to me—someone who believed in me and had faith in me.

CHAPTER 19

Getting Fired

I had a good couple of years in the developmental league from 2006–2008. I called myself G-Rilla and I was basically a street thug. My first match was in September and I defeated Big Bully Douglas. A month later I became the enforcer for Urban Assault, which was a tag team made up of Eric Pérez and Sonny Siaki. In January 2007, I formed a tag team with Freakin' Deacon and we had a good run together defeating many well-known teams including Frankie Coverdale and Bob Hoskins, the Samoan fight club, Shawn Osborne and Jon Bolen, and Robert Anthony and Johnny Curtis. In June 2007 I made my debut at FCW's inaugural show and I defeated Shawn Osborne. Things continued going well for me. For a short while, I briefly formed a tag team with Robert Anthony and then something happened. I was very far from the big time, but I was making my way. I wasn't on television yet, but audiences seemed to like me. But then the bottom dropped out.

To this day, I am mystified about why I got released from my wrestling contract. We had wrapped up the operation in McDonough and moved down to Tampa, Florida. There was a whole new facility being built there, and we were the ones helping to get it started. Me and a bunch of the other wrestlers had started having a Texas hold 'em poker night on Tuesdays. Just something to pass the time. I thought my star was rising within the ranks and things were looking up. But evidently, that wasn't the case. Once we got our poker night together, I called the office and made a request for three fold-out chairs that we could use during the game. Not a big deal. I showed up at the office, I took the chairs along with a bunch of DVD wrestling box sets that were really cool. Just the kind of stuff I love watching. Binge watching before the term even existed. Anyway, the next day I got a call from Steve Keirn, another former wrestler who worked for WWE. He said to me, bluntly, "Why did you steal those three chairs?" I didn't know what the fuck he was talking about. Steal three chairs? He was angry about it. We went back and forth and I told him that I was very pissed off at being accused of being a thief. He seemed to understand where I was coming from, and we left it there.

That was Super Bowl weekend, and the next day my Patriots were playing the Giants. I thought that Patriots were one of the greatest teams to ever exist and yet they lost and it crushed me. We were off on Mondays, so I was headed to the gym to work out when I got a call from Ty Bailey, another WWE exec. He told me that "Things were not working out" and that they were going to release me. I asked him what the hell he was talking about, and he said he didn't want to get into it. Did it have something to do with those chairs? Maybe that was just the excuse they used. I had only one house show under my belt at that point, so I guess I was easy to let go. Of course, my first thought was that it was because I was Black. But that's just where I was back then. I know Steve is not a racist. But I was very confused. Obviously, there were people in the organization that didn't want me there, and I think they used the chair episode to get rid of me. Either way, that was that. There was nothing I could do. I packed my bags and drove back to California. When I got back, I called Keys and said "Can you help me?" He said, "Of course. I'll get you back to work right away." And so that was the end of my wrestling career. Or at least that's what I thought.

CHAPTER 20

Starting Over

Once I got back to Southern California after being let go by the WWE, I started working again right out of the gate as a bodyguard. That was my fallback position. I was good at it and the money was decent, so it was a no-brainer. Around this time in Los Angeles, there was a guy named TK who was the king of the party throwers. A guru. This was the era of pop-up parties—spontaneous, A-list, makeshift extravaganzas that could happen anywhere, from an abandoned building down-town to a private club in Hollywood. And TK knew how to get it done. He was somehow related to Los Angeles Lakers owner Jerry Buss and he had also been a professional choreographer. He was another bigger-than-life Los Angeles character, and, thankfully, he was tight with my old friend Rico, the bouncer from my previous life at the Saddle Ranch Chop House. Rico put in a good word for me, and all of a sudden, I was working for TK. He was a cool guy. He knew my reputation and he was happy to have me aboard, so that felt good. He was just blowing up at the time. Anybody who was anybody wanted to get into a party thrown by TK. And so, obviously, these were the hardest parties to get into around town.

TK's behavior was somewhat effeminate, but he was a total player with the ladies. He was the star around town and everybody knew it; he was a magnet for some of the most beautiful women I've ever seen. Around this time, Suge Knight was the biggest Hollywood gangster, and he would show up at many of TK's get-togethers. It was like throwing a big shark in the water when he would show up. Everybody got nervous but was still fascinated in his presence.

During this time, TK "discovered" an up-and-coming rapper named Game and would host performance parties to help his career. He was trying to push Game's career all the way up. One night, Suge came in with his crew and TK got nervous because he didn't want any trouble. He knew that if Suge knew that an up-and-coming rapper was in the house, things could get out of control pretty quickly. That's because Game was already working with Dr. Dre and TK knew that Suge might do whatever he could to get him over to Death Row Records, which Suge ran. Dre had been a cofounder of Death Row back in 1992 but by now had left to form his own label, so things were tense. I hustled the rapper out of there fast when I saw Suge, which TK totally respected. He just didn't want trouble.

Working TK's parties could be a challenge, given all of the A-listers that would show up. I remember one night at one of the parties in Hollywood, Jerry Buss and his crew were getting bottle service at a table. Mike Tyson came in with his crew and took a table nearby. Then Gwen Stefani came in and grabbed another table nearby. You had very big names in many of these situations, and I had to be on my toes as a bodyguard/bouncer.

I really liked Tyson. Sweet guy, always paid for everybody with him. It always looked like he was being taken advantage of. At least to my eyes. He was very soft-spoken, a real gentleman in these situations. And you could just see his crew taking advantage of him left and right.

TK parties were a glimpse into the belly of the beast of Hollywood celebrity. I would watch the party, and also, oftentimes, I was taking care of TK directly. But one night he pulled me aside and said, "We have somebody big coming in tonight you need to be aware of. Prince is coming in."

Okay, well, that was pretty cool. Who didn't like Prince? When His Royal Badness arrived, I couldn't help but notice how small he was. Literally, it was like I could pick him up and put him in my pocket. He was just absolutely tiny. He was wearing an earring in the shape of that new symbol he had become after doing battle with his record company over royalties. When the earring fell out and dropped to the floor, TK was right on it, snatched it up, and presented it back to Prince. Rather than accept it, Prince said "It's okay, I don't need it." TK whispered to me, "It must be costume jewelry." Prince heard him, grinned a little bit, and said, "Prince don't wear no costume jewelry, baby. Just keep it." Badass.

Another thing that struck me about Prince was how deep his voice was. I mean, it was really, really low. He stayed for a little while and then left with his entourage. A few nights later, we got word that Prince was coming back to another one of TK's parties. TK was ready with a big private table and bottle service all set to go. TK told me, "Look, he's coming in with his own security and they are cool, but I need a big guy like you to make sure everybody gets what they need, okay?"

"No problem, boss," I said. "I'll do whatever you need."

Prince arrived that night and, sure enough, he had his own crew—but they were cool guys. You could tell he hired total professionals. Nobody was fucking around, and nobody was paying attention to the celebrities. They were all about keeping an eye on the prize—in this case, Prince. Prince remembered me and asked how I was doing; I told him I was good and he nodded and gave me a little smile.

Later that night, one of Prince's bodyguards came over to me and said, "Prince would like a word with you." I couldn't figure out what was going on. I'd been keeping my eye on him all night from a pretty good distance because, again, he had a good team around him. Either way, I went over to Prince and he motioned for me to bend down so I could hear him. In that deep voice, he said in my ear, "Do you know why I'm successful?"

I thought for a quick moment and said, "Because you play guitar and sing good?"

Prince shook his head and said, "It's because I dedicate myself to God."

I said, "Okay." I mean, whatever floats your boat, right?

But Prince wasn't finished. He continued, "Would you be willing to do that? Would you be willing to dedicate yourself to God one day a week?" I didn't want to disrespect Prince; I knew he was a Jehovah's Witness, and I'm not one to judge someone's religious persuasions. He said, "I might have some work for you if you're interested." I nodded and said politely, "Thank you, Prince. I'll think about that." And that was that. A little while after that, he motioned me over again and said, "I'm ready to go." His bodyguards seemed cool to let me take the lead, so I began escorting him out of the club. Guiding him out, I noticed right away that people were starting to push in to get a piece of Prince. He was such a small guy, I got concerned that the crush of the crowd could injure him—not that anybody was *trying* to hurt him, but it might've happened by accident. So I did the only thing that made sense: I picked him up and basically put him on my hip like a three-year-old and began walking him through the crowd. I could hear his bodyguards behind me snickering, but what the fuck, this was the only way to get it done. Mike Tyson was there and he looked over and took in the whole scene, as did Busta Rhymes. For me, it was just another night of interesting craziness. I did get Prince out to his car, however.

When I got back in the club an argument had started brewing and I saw somebody getting physical with TK. I snapped right back into being his personal bodyguard and took this guy, wrapped my arm around his neck, and put him to sleep in about five seconds. He woke up again a few moments later and when that happens, it's like they reboot when they wake up. They come to with an entirely different state of mind. And they know they can't be fucking around like that.

I was having a good time working with TK and it was never boring, as you can probably imagine. I got to see some really interesting things. But in the back of my mind, I kept thinking about what Snoop and Keys said to me before I left to be a wrestler. I wasn't quite sure if they truly meant that door was always open, but I thought it would be worth giving it a test. I had really liked working for Snoop and, as crazy and interesting is the club scene was, it was exhausting and often filled with too much drama for my blood. I was still willing to do some part-time bodyguarding on the club scene, but I was very happy when I called Keys and he said, "We'd love to have you back. Snoop trusts and respects you and I know he'll be happy to have you back on the team." I got the call a few days later that Snoop had officially given it a green light, and a couple of days after that they put me on the schedule. My first assignment was to go keep an eye on Snoop when he was coaching his youth football league.

I was well aware of the nonprofit organization that Snoop had founded just a couple of years earlier, in 2005. Not just because I was a football fan, but because everybody knew about what he had done. It was bigger than football. The goal of the Snoop Youth Football League (SYFL) was to take kids between the ages of five and thirteen and teach them the values of teamwork, good sportsmanship, discipline, and self-respect while also reminding them how important school is. The first year he started the league, more than thirteen hundred kids in the Los Angeles area took part. He got the kids uniforms that looked like they were straight out of the NFL. The season included seven regular-season games and then a three-week playoff concluding with a Super Bowl at the end of November. He even had all-star teams that were chosen and so certain players got to travel to Houston, Texas, each year. It was incredibly organized and well run. The other thing I liked about Snoop's football league was that it provided for kids regardless of race, color, creed, or economic background. It wasn't about any of that stuff. Race especially had nothing to do with it. It was strictly about giving all kids a chance to learn the values of character, integrity, discipline, and teamwork through football. It brought communities together, it helped families, and, most of all, it helped young players get on a path where they would become strong, decent, positive young men. So I was a huge fan of that program. How could you not be? Snoop isn't one of those guys who does things to get attention for himself. He does it because he thinks it's the right thing to do. I could tell that in those first few months that I worked with him. Sometimes people think because of what they see in the videos or what they hear in the music that Snoop is one kind of guy. But Snoop has many facets to his personality, including being a great family man and a supporter for those in need.

CHAPTER 21

Football Coach

When I went to the SYFL practice fields in Panorama City out in the San Fernando Valley, I was completely blown away by the organization. I had played enough football to know what it's like when an organization is quality, and this was beyond the scope of any youth football league I ever could have imagined. The fields were well maintained, the equipment was top notch, and there was a sense of order to the operation. In the back of my mind, I kept thinking how valuable a league like this could have been for me when I was a young kid. It was a lot different being on the sidelines of a practice field bodyguarding for Snoop that it was in a place like the Staples Center, where everybody was trying to get a piece of him. This was far more low-key and relaxed. I'm sure most of the kids didn't even really know who he was or how major a celebrity he was. He was just a guy who ran the league. And coached.

You could tell that rapper Kelly "K-Mac" Garmon was Snoop's right-hand man when it came to coaching. He and Snoop were having lots of private dialogues, and you could tell there was a lot of trust there. Given that there wasn't much for me to do as a bodyguard in this situation, my eyes kept wandering over to the kids playing football on the field. At one point I couldn't resist. I said to one of the kids, showing him how to guard, "Use your hands to make a diamond shape, like this." Some of the other kids overheard me and came over to hear what I was saying. K-Mac noticed and made some good-natured cracks about me trying to coach. "I know something about football," I said to him.

K-Mac had been part of a gangster rap duo from Lynnwood, California, called "The Comrads." He and "Gangsta" Terrell Anderson started blowing up in the summer of 1997 with the single "Homeboyz." That's what launched them. He had also appeared in some movies, and I'm sure many of you got to know K-Mac watching Netflix in 2018 when they dedicated an entire series to Snoop's football league.

I didn't want to encroach on the relationship became K-Mac and Snoop, but I just couldn't resist helping those kids out on the football field. I was good at working with kids, and I never thought for a second that Snoop was in any kind of danger down there on the field. It may sound like I was violating my bodyguard policy of never taking your eyes off the client, but those were special circumstances down there. K-Mac said something to me like, "You think you're pretty good? You think you could do something with these kids?"

I said to him, "Give me five guys. Let me work with five guys and you'll see what I'm talking about."

And he said no problem. Snoop didn't seem to mind either, and so I was relieved of my bodyguarding responsibilities. They grabbed someone else from the crew, and all of a sudden, I was coaching football for Snoop. I didn't waste a minute. I had the kids laughing right away, teaching them "don't trust anybody on the field" and "receivers are only going to try and steal your girlfriend." "You trust guys on the line and that's it." I said to them, "You want to be like John Wayne out there." One wise-guy kid said, "Ain't he the guy that wouldn't hire Black people?" I said, "For our purposes, he was a badass who stood up to the bad guys." I showed them how to do pigeon toes and diamonds with their hands and I gave all the kids nicknames. My offensive line was committed to being the best on the field if it was the last thing we did. K-Mac would be screaming at his defensive line while I was whipping the offensive line into shape.

Snoop must've liked what was happening out there because pretty soon the bodyguarding schedule was completely changed and I was booked full-time as a coach, not a bodyguard. The more I got to see of the organization, the more impressed I was. Snoop would hire buses to get the kids to games, he gave them the best uniforms to wear, and he made it like a professional experience for them. These kids couldn't believe what it was like to play for Snoop. During the games, if one of the kids I was coaching missed a block, Snoop would shoot me a look. He took his football seriously, that's for sure. K-Mac would do the same thing. I think it was making K-Mac a little nervous out there, because game after game, the offensive was outperforming the defensive line. Most importantly, though, the kids were getting great lessons and having a lot of fun. I started thinking that I didn't want to bodyguard anymore, that I would just love to be a full-time youth football coach. It was just that rewarding.

Our team had a good season and, at the end of each year, Snoop hosted a big awards ceremony to say thank you to the many volunteers that helped him run his nonprofit. When it was time for the announcement of who was going to receive the Coach of the Year Award, I just assumed it was going to be Snoop. He was a great coach and everybody knew it. But when the envelope was opened it was actually Snoop who read the words, "This year's most valuable coach is George Murdoch." I looked down. I kept waiting for the other shoe to fall, thinking this might be all part of some ball-busting practical joke. But nobody was laughing. Everybody—from the kids to be adults—were clapping as hard as they could. I almost couldn't walk up to the podium I was so stunned. Once I got up there, I tried to crack a joke by calling out the fact that my name was spelled wrong on the trophy. Everybody laughed, but I had tears in my eyes. This was probably the greatest thing I'd ever experienced up until that point in my life. It was so special because I never had any idea I was even in the running. Come on, I was a bodyguard who offered a couple of tips and got lucky when they gave me a shot on the field. K-Mac, Snoop, and I had a great friendship. I owe those guys so much for bringing me in as they did. That was a game changer for me. To know that people had faith in me like that and respected me and trusted me with young people made a huge difference in my life.

CHAPTER 22

𝔅ack on the 𝔍oad

𝖀nce the youth football season ended, Snoop was adamant that I get back to my bodyguarding duties with him. We had bonded, and he had not forgotten what my attitude was like on the road—and he was about to embark on some of the most ambitious, grueling tour schedules of his life.

For months, our feet barely touched the ground. Literally just a week or so after the season was over, we left and hit every place from Australia, multiple trips around Europe, Amsterdam, Norway, and then into St. Petersburg, Russia. It was simply mind-boggling how much travel we were doing. And everywhere we went, Snoop was received like royalty. You think he's big in the United States? Try walking down the street with him in London or Paris or Oslo. All hell breaks loose. I don't speak any foreign languages, so my one-liners were lost on many folks around the world—but I think they got my attitude. Russia was probably the craziest. There was always something going on while we were there: shady guys trying to sneak backstage and, one night when I got on the tour bus after a show, there was a guy whom I didn't recognize sitting there. For starters, he was a white guy, so he stood out like a piece of chalk. I said, "Who are you?" He said, "I'm Corrupt." *What?* I knew who Corrupt was. He was one of Snoop's background singers. How the hell did *this* guy ever get on the bus? It wasn't on my watch but I still took care of it, picking him up by the neck and throwing him out of the door. That's when Snoop showed up and wanted to know what happened. He got a kick out of how I handled that.

On another night, Snoop was performing at a club and there was a roped-off VIP section for us to hang out in. It was a fucking zoo up there—way too many people—but the Russians didn't care about that. They packed in as many as they could. I don't think there are any fire laws over there. A couple of guys who were supposedly with the Russian mafia showed up and wanted to meet Snoop. I told them to get the hell out of our space and one of the guys stepped back and produced a silver-plated .45. I still said to them, "No dice; get the hell out of here," all the while keeping my cool. I wasn't looking to take a bullet, believe me. But I know that when a guy produces a gun, he's usually just showing it, sort of like a peacock strutting with his feathers out. If he wants to shoot you, he's going to take it out and just shoot you. At least that had always been my experience back home. Keys came in later and couldn't believe what was going on.

There were plenty of other episodes over in Russia when I had to manhandle guys for trying to pierce the barrier between me and Snoop. I mean, I had to kick some emcee's ass one night and I'm sure the guy wasn't a troublemaker, but he was too persistent about getting close to Snoop. People had to understand I was being paid to protect this guy. There was nothing fun and games about it. I really don't give a fuck about your drama or that you really want to meet Snoop. Everybody wants to meet Snoop. If Snoop met every single person that desired to have a moment with him, he wouldn't have time for anything else.

Another night someplace in Russia, I forget the exact city, this young Russian guy came backstage, saying to me that he was Russia's bestselling rapper and he just had to meet with Snoop. I said he's not seeing anybody right now and that guy said, "This is my country. You're a guest in my country, and if you don't let me in there is going to be a problem." I said, "Okay, come on, I'll take you to see Snoop." We were walking back by catering and off to the side was a curtain. I said, "Come on. Snoop is right here; right this way, my good friend." I opened the curtain and threw him down that staircase into the darkness. I don't care what county I am in; I have no time for bullshit like that.

I lost my job for a moment in Amsterdam. We had a little break there—some time off one day—so Kevin and I went to enjoy some of their famous "coffee" shops. Kevin and I always had a bond of friendship. He's just a real person and is sarcastic and loves dark humor. We hit it off from the jump and soon became a team. Oftentimes I'd work more with Kevin than with the other bodyguards. We also shared a love of sports. Kev is a die-hard Toronto Maple Leafs fan and anyone claiming that, I respect. That is like being a Jets fan...only a real fan would claim that. We had a lot of adventures together on the road with Snoop. The biggest thing we had in common was he respected the job. We did our job. We weren't fans or "marcs" as we'd say in pro wrestling, slang for super-obsessed fanatics. We didn't want photo ops with Snoop. When we got down time, we'd sneak off and do our own thing. We didn't hover around Snoop. He had his friends. We were not his friends. We worked for him. Yes, there's a respect and you can like your boss, but he's always your boss. The biggest mistake a bodyguard or manager can make, as I've said, is getting too comfortable and forgetting the job. So I never smoked with Snoop because I couldn't do my job high. Even coaching with Snoop, he was the head coach; I was a position coach. We weren't buddies, coaching together. In working with celebrities, you have to maintain professionalism, and when you don't, people get hurt, fired, or worse.

With this mindset, Kevin and I—on our off time—would go to baseball games, restaurants, movies, whatever we could get into. In Amsterdam, it was the same thing. We wanted to go to a "coffee" shop. Snoop had an appearance at a "coffee" shop at one. We took him to the place, and he was given his choice of greens from every corner of the globe...and he and his friends had fun. Kevin and I decided we'd come back when we got off work. And we did, and I picked out a strain called "white lighting" and then noticed they also had some delicious-looking pie! Yes, please! Two slices. Kevin got a slice and we sat down and did like everyone anywhere: bitched about work, complained about life—which was fun for us. And I had no idea edibles were a thing. We couldn't stop laughing and we were making plans to find beer and food next when the door opened and Snoop and the team were coming back for more.

I was technically off the clock but Kevin never was, and, in reality, neither was I, but maybe it was the moon pie talking. I was high and wasn't going to work on my break time. Kevin wanted to leave and I was all, "Hell, no! I'm finishing my pie." And I did! Huge rebellion on my part. We got up, the munchies hit hard, and the hazy high melted any filter I had on my inner monologue. As we walked by Snoop, I noticed he had on a track suit and a slingshot tank top. I made a joke about how he looked. Hilarious. As I walked out of the shop, I realized Kevin hadn't walked out with me. I was about to go back for Kevin but I saw a majestic Burger King sign and like a chubby moth to the flame I was drawn to two double whoppers and a chocolate shake! And I devoured everything. Then I started walking back to the shop but I saw a bar with a piano player singing American songs, so I wandered over and they had beer in giant mugs! I was in! Within ten minutes, I was singing Neil Diamond's "Sweet Caroline" with my new best friends, an old German piano player who loved classic rock 'n' roll and groups of people from all over. We drank beer in harmony and sang out of key. Dogs howled better, but no matter. It was fun! I eventually returned to the hotel, got to my room, and I still had about five hours before my shift started back.

Keys, who was on the door, looked at me with concern. "Hey, G, you okay?"

I said, "Yeah, we had some fun and oh! I brought you some pie." I was going to tell him it was "magic pie" but he interrupted me.

"They going to book you a flight tomorrow, okay?"

I said, "Why, we going home early?"

"No. Snoop fired you."

I said, "For what?" He said the coffee shop joke! "Shhhhh-hhhit yeah, that was funny." I was still high so I took the news very laid-back and accepting. "Okay, well, you want to get rest then. I'll pack and stay on the door for you." Keys said thanks and that he'd talk to Dogg and straighten it out. I said, "No, it's all good." And I started packing.

143

About two hours later the door opened. It was Snoop. I was standing across from his room, in my room with the door open. He said, "Hey, can you get me some room service? I'm starving. What you packing for?"

"You fired me," I said.

Snoop said, "When?"

I said, "At the coffee shop."

Snoop said "We went to a coffee shop?"

I said, "Did we?"

"Food, G...and unpack!"

Ah, the power of weed!

As the tour continued wrapping around the world, we wound up on the outskirts of Toronto, where Snoop was going to perform at an outdoor festival on this beautiful lake. It was the inaugural 1000 Islands Music Fest in Gananoque, in August of 2009.

One thing about Snoop that I don't think he would mind me sharing with you is that he is not crazy about animals at all. Just not his thing. And where we were staying on that lake was a gorgeous natural setting, really beautiful and rustic. I loved it. But Snoop's not a real outdoorsy kind of guy either. And there were lots of animals, especially these black squirrels that seemed to be everyplace. Supposedly there were also black bears wandering around, but when we got there, it was all about the squirrels. They put us all in these bomb-ass cabins that were really beautiful. Once in a while, when bodyguarding for Snoop, I would get a perk like that.

I was on break for several hours and my buddy, the bassist in the band, said, "Let's go out on the lake in a couple of canoes." Kevin was also going to come along. Now, my buddy and I both had kind of a weight problem and that canoe was moaning in agony as we took this little trip around the lake. We could see moose walking around on the mountain and it was just incredible: relaxing, scenic, and a really nice change of pace after all of the globetrotting craziness we had just been through. When we got back to shore, I started feeding the squirrels these peanut M&Ms, which were like crack for them. They were just going off, following me like I was the Pied Piper. Snoop popped his head out of the cabin and was not impressed by the squirrels. "These are black squirrels, dog," I said to him, "Are you racist?" He laughed and said, "Look, man, I'm not feeling too good about all this out here. Keep a close eye on my cabin, okay? I don't do animals." Me, I was like Dr. Doolittle out there, but Snoop wanted none of it, so I just promised him I'd keep a close eye.

The next day, Snoop opened the door of his cabin and learned that during the night, a black bear had been too close for comfort for him. Snoop had had enough. We only had one more night at the cabin, but he was out of there. "I'm taking me a helicopter to fly into a nice hotel in Toronto. You motherfuckers can have this! I'll see you at the show!" After he was gone, we had a blast waterskiing and doing some more things in the great outdoors. Again, a really nice perk that we sometimes got to experience.

This exhausting tour was finally going to be winding down in Jacksonville, Florida. Kevin was also a die-hard wrestling fan, and he told me excitedly that Snoop was going to appear at a WWE match. Well, to be honest, I didn't like the sound of that. I had been unceremoniously cut loose by the WWE, and I didn't want to get embarrassed by seeing anybody I used to know and work with. It was the only time ever working for

Snoop that this happened—where I just didn't feel up to going to an event. I explained my dilemma to Kevin and he was very understanding, but he also said to me, "Listen, I think you're overthinking this. I could easily switch you out with another bodyguard. But I don't think that's the right thing to do. You're a good man, you have a great place with us, and you should go there and hold your head up. Fuck those guys. Their loss. I don't think you should worry about this." I appreciated his supportive words, but I still wasn't feeling it. Evidently, Kevin spoke to Snoop about it and before we got to Jacksonville, he pulled me aside as well and said, "Man, you're good. You're part of this. They made a mistake with you and I agree with Kevin. Walk into that place like you belong. They got nothing on you." These guys looked at the situation in a different way, and I really appreciated it.

When we got to the arena that night, walking through the parking lot after getting out of the limo, I saw Cody Rhodes, Dusty's son. Normally, of course, we would've exchanged pleasantries. He was a good guy and his father meant the world to me. I hadn't seen Cody in a long time, either, so there was lots to talk about. Cody was really nice, and he came over and said, "What's up man!" But I stopped him; I put my head down and kept walking with Snoop. Kevin was like, "Goddamn, man. That was pretty cold."

We got to the arena and I saw some of the old WWE crew there to welcome Snoop. When Tommy Dreamer saw me, he did a double take. I didn't know what he was going to say, but he walked over to me and said quietly, "Hey, if you don't mind, I would like to talk with you a little bit later if you have a free moment, okay? I just want to clear the air."

"No problem," I said, and I kept hustling Snoop through the layers of doors until we got to his dressing room. I couldn't imagine what John wanted to talk to me about specifically, but hey, clearing the air is always a good thing. I'm all about that.

I was anxious to hear what he had to say. Later on, once Snoop went out to do his thing in front of the crowd, I had a bit of a break and that's when John caught up with me. "Listen to me," he said, "I've just got to come out and say it. We made a mistake. I did not have all the information when you were let go. That's on me. I think you are tremendously talented. You have a great size, great look, and you have an amazing personality. Why don't we try this again? Would you be up for that?"

I almost couldn't believe what I was hearing. I was actually dumbstruck, and that doesn't happen a lot to me. I said to him, "Listen, I really appreciate what you're saying. Can I think about it for a couple of weeks? I'm happy with what I'm doing right now and I'm still kind of stunned over what happened with you guys. But I do want to think about it."

"You take all the time you need," he said.

Well, this was some serious food for thought. What was I going to do? Wrestling had long been my dream; I had had a shot, and then had it taken away for me. I had found a new path in life. I loved the adventures, I loved the football, I loved the entourage, and I loved the money. I loved everything about it. But how long was this Snoop bodyguarding gig really going to go on? Another couple of years? I did a lot of soul-searching after we flew back home. I had a bodyguarding job in Phoenix, and John called me again to restate his offer. "I need to know what you're doing," he said.

After thinking long and hard, I decided that I couldn't pass up the opportunity. Inside, I really wanted to be my own guy. With Snoop, I was always good to be that guy in the background that you would see in pictures. The bodyguard. But I guess I wanted more than that. When I got back to California, I sat down with Kevin and explained to him what I was thinking. And then Snoop came in the room and we talked about it. "Listen," Snoop said. "You're a great coach and you're a great bodyguard. You can always do those things again if you want. If you've learned anything working for me it's that I want everybody around me to be successful. You have to do what you need to do. Like I told you last time, if doesn't work out I'm here for you. But I think it's going to work out for you. This is your destiny, man. You can't pass this up."

CHAPTER 23

Back to the WWE (2010)

I knew Snoop was right about pursuing wrestling again, and I realized I'd probably never be his bodyguard again. But we would be friends. There was definitely a unique bond formed between Snoop and me, and to this day we remain tight. Being around him taught me a lot about life, about business, and about people. Snoop is a great teacher and he doesn't even know it. I mean, he doesn't consider himself a teacher. But if you watch him closely, if you're lucky enough to be in his presence and you watch how he runs his life, you know the guy is special. When he tells you something is the right thing to be doing, that's as powerful an endorsement as you're ever going to get. As a gag going-away gift, he got me a Celtics coloring book and some shitty crayons after a trip he made to Boston. I hear that Ice Cube gave his bodyguards new cars, but Snoop wasn't about presents. The gift was what you learned from him. And I'll never be able to put a value on what I learned from Snoop Dogg.

I drove to Tampa from Burbank. I had been traveling the world with Snoop, which meant we ate late, we ate often, and we ate bad. When I had last left the WWE, I weighed about 343 pounds. When I got back to Florida and hopped up on the scale, I was at 487. Dr. Tom Prichard said to me seriously, "It looks like we have some work to do." I knew I could do it; it was just going to take some time. I started making a dent in my weight and Rob MacIntyre was incredibly helpful with that. Steve Keirn, the guy I had the argument with over the stolen chairs, saw me and just said quietly, "Welcome back."

By that time, the facility in Tampa was fully functioning as the "School of Hard Knocks" and it was actually very inspiring. Many greats came through: old-school legends left and right. It was so helpful to have all those agents and managers around there who could give you great, critical advice on what you needed to do to grow. I was picking the brains of the greatest wrestlers in the world—especially Dusty Rhodes. He was really my guy. I was working my ass off. I soon got back down to 356 pounds and I was getting stronger. I scored the second-highest bench-pressing weight ever at Hard Knocks, and in January 2010, I re-signed with WWE and, shortly after that, was assigned back to FCW. I was still using the name G-Rilla, but not for long. In a couple of months, I changed my ring name to Brodus Clay, a play on Snoop Dogg's actual name, which was Calvin Broadus. I had to give my buddy a little shout-out. Snoop had been so supportive of my life and my career that I thought it would be a nice homage to base my name on him.

CHAPTER 24

Funkasaurus (2012–2013)

In 2012, I took a few months off to appear in a movie called *No One Lives*, directed by the Japanese filmmaker Ryuhei Kitamura. He and I totally hit it off, and I wanted to talk to him about the Godzilla movies he had worked on. Working on *No One Lives* was a fun experience for me. We shot down in Covington, Louisiana, and I got to appear in a very cool fight scene. It was fun appearing in a horror film, even though making movies involves lots of standing around (or sitting around in trailers) doing nothing. In the WWE, you never stopped moving, and making movies was the exact opposite. I got antsy and I got anxious and I couldn't wait to return to the ring. But little did I know that my days as a heel, a heel called Brodus Clay, were numbered.

When I was told I was going to be the "Funkasaurus," I didn't think it was going to work. I did not think I could pull it off.

Once I got back from making the movie, I was running vignettes for Brodus Clay, this murderous villain, and my story was, when I beat an opponent, I took things from them.

I got the idea from watching the film *Bloodsport*. After Bolo Yeung beat Jean-Claude Van Damme, he took his handkerchief and crushed it. As a kid, I loved that. It was like the ultimate disrespect. I thought it was really entertaining. I pitched this idea to the team—that I would have a "house of pain" where I would collect all these different items from guys that I defeated. Triple H and Stephanie loved the idea, so we ran with it. There was always lots of anticipation about what I would take from a guy when I beat him. So things were going great. It was a hot character and I think it was considered successful. Then one time backstage I was cracking jokes, and the kingpin, Vince McMahon, heard me. He started laughing at my jokes and commented, "Are we sure this guy is a heel? Because he's pretty damn funny."

Uh oh, I thought. Anybody who knows Vince McMahon's history knows that he loves to sing and dance, and honestly, dancing was the last thing I wanted to do up there in the ring. But I kind of sensed what was coming. The real reason I didn't want to do it is I thought of the stigma of being up there, a Black man, shucking and jiving. Plus, I wasn't a dancer. That said, some of the greatest wrestlers of all time had been dancers up there. Jimmy Valiant, Thunderbolt Patterson, and of course my personal hero and mentor, Dusty Rhodes.

I was confused and a little concerned when it came back to me that Vince wanted me to be a dancer in the ring. So I went to Dusty because I trusted him and asked him what he thought I should do. He looked at me as if to say, "What's the problem?" Then he started talking. "You know my history! You're a historian! If I could get up there and do it, why can't you do it?" Then he started dancing around the room and I started laughing my head off. It was just what I needed to see to start considering the next phase of my wrestling career.

At that point I needed to create a new character because Vince wanted me up there dancing and being funny. He saw something in me that spoke to him when it came to humor and entertainment. He didn't like me as much as a heel as he did a potential funnyman. Being the wrestling historian that I am, I knew there was potential there for me. Even though Brodus Clay was a hot character, it wasn't hot enough to get me on television in a big way, and this new direction seemed to have some potential. I told the powers that be that I wanted a little bit of time to go back down to Florida and work with Dusty Rhodes and they said no problem. So Dusty and I started working together. He put on the song "Moves Like Jagger" and, like I said, started jumping around the room like a crazy sonofabitch. That just cracked me up. I couldn't believe he wanted me to do that, but then he finally said to me, "Come on, you want to make money for your family, don't you? What the heck are you waiting for? Get the hell out here and start dancing." And then I did, and I started laughing again, and I realized he was just giving me permission to believe. He was making being a dancer fun and he was making it silly and he was making it acceptable for me. He was being a great mentor. But I created this crazy, dancing character with a clear under-standing that no matter how much fun and silly Dusty made it for me, I still couldn't really dance. I am simply not a dancer. So these two girls Naomi and Ariane helped me out, and they became part of the team.

Naomi was the best athlete in WWE developmental and was just waiting for an opportunity to go to main roster *Raw* or *SmackDown*, and Ariane was new and coming off a *Tough*

Enough WWE reality show where she was the first one eliminated but had made the biggest impression. They were working on their own characters and team. Naomi (real name Trinity Fatu) was a former Orlando Magic cheerleader/dancer and we both were in the same boat trying to get our spots on the main roster. I said to my mentor, "Dusty, I need help with this dancing, it's not my thing."

Dusty smiled and said, "You need some professional help, baby, and I saw them working on some stuff in the ring."

I looked at Dusty and said, "Naomi could be my choreographer!"

Dusty said, "What about Ariane? A dance team? Yes!"

Sitting in the office, Dusty and me figured it out; they go out and dance great as my sidekicks and I could just do my thing—but no one will watch me! Brilliant!"

The question became, would the girls go for it? I went to them, and, to my surprise, they said "Yes!" But it was a dance team with the goal that they would eventually branch out as a tag team wrestling duo but this was the roster spot. I was so thankful Naomi took what I considered a step back to be a Funkadactyl (along with Ariane), but she did and I was set!

All of a sudden, I had a tiny bit of swagger. I'd got at least a couple of moves in my pocket. By then it was time to have a name for the character. At first, I wanted to be "Heavy G," but Heavy D had just died and so that didn't seem to make sense. I did not want any confusion when it came to that. So I was working out in the gym with Rob MacIntyre. He's a super influential guy in my life who has always had a positive influence on me. And we were just talking about my new character needing a name. Out of the blue, from nowhere, he says to me, "What about Funkasaurus?" I thought that sounded kind of funny and I said to him "Okay, let's work with that. What planet am I from? I can't be from Planet X because that's where I just came from with my last character. And he said to me, "How about Planet Funk?" And that was it. The Funkasaurus was born. And the two hot girls, Naomi and Ariane, became my sexy sidekicks, the "Funkadactyls."

So then it was time to get the show on the road. It was time to launch that new show and new character. Dusty pulled me aside not long before the first match and he whispered to me, "Listen, I know you're not comfortable doing this. I know it feels out of your range. But you're good. You're really good. When you get out there and smell that popcorn, and you hear that crowd, you are going to know what to do. I've taught you everything. You are like me out there. Nobody has more faith in you than I do. You get out there and you do what we both know you can do, okay?"

It wasn't just Dusty who had my back. A bunch of other veterans who had done similar characters would all come up to me and tell me that I was doing great, and that I was doing the right thing. Michael Hayes, one of the great legends, took me aside and showed me how to make my entrance. I mean one of the greatest hall of famers of all time and he was letting me know that he believed in me. Other guys were volunteering to be my debut match. It was pretty cool to realize and experience the kind of faith they had in me. When Brian Myers said to Triple H, "I would really want to be his first match," that meant a lot to me. Everybody had my back, it seemed.

The only one that seemed to have an issue with it was Undertaker. He said to me, "Do yourself a favor; when you get out there, just take a fall and it will all be over."

I said, "What are you talking about?"

He said, "I don't think you need a gimmick."

I said, "Are you kidding me? Being 'Undertaker' isn't a gimmick? When you go out there with lipstick and mascara, that's not a gimmick?"

His reply? "Well, I just do what I'm told."

I said, "So what's the difference? That's all I'm doing!" In hindsight, I think I know what he was talking about. He really didn't think I needed a gimmick. He thought I was a good heel and that they were just trying to put lipstick on a bull. I actually respect and appreciate it now, but back then I didn't really get it. I think I was too caught up in what was happening around me.

When it was time to debut my new character and act, Triple H pulled me aside and said, "Whatever you do, after it's all done, don't look at the internet." Originally, I was supposed to start in Memphis, but things kept getting pushed back while we refined everything, so the first night I went out it was actually in Corpus Christi, Texas. I have to say that by delaying it eight, nine, or ten times like they did, they built up a lot of mystery and anticipation. The buzz was off the chart. Everybody was expecting a monster. That's the kind of reputation I had established up until then. Nobody had any idea what this new character was going to be like, and I was very impressed with how that created the buzz that it did.

So we got there for the first night and everybody was there. My agent, Road Dogg, was running around all excited. He knew the new act had potential. I would be taking on Brian Myers, so it would be a decent match. And there was Vince McMahon sitting in his chair. That made me nervous. It's hard to even describe what Vince McMahon is to wrestling. Most other professional sports—and yes, wrestling is a professional sport—don't have a figure as powerful or important as Vince McMahon. I mean, this is the guy that came up with WWE. This is the ultimate boss. Without him, there is no professional wrestling as we know it today. He's the father who created all of our dreams. When I think about life before WrestleMania, it was a different world. WrestleMania made everything bigger than life. The characters, the drama, the stories…I don't think there will ever be anything else ever that matches the sheer drama and entertainment of WrestleMania.

And so there he was, just sitting there. He was a mysterious figure to me. When you first meet him, he just looks you over, looks you up and down, and sizes you up. He's intimidating. You never quite know what he's thinking. And then, just like that, once you start working for him, he loosens up; he's breaking your balls and he's simply one of the greatest guys on the planet. Brutally honest, but also brutally funny. That said, he's still the boss. If he doesn't like something, it goes away. But if he does like something, then your life has the possibility to change for the better. Much better. Vince McMahon knows who he is and what he wants. I would hear him say to people, "I don't like it." They would say, "What don't you like?" He would fire back, "Everything!" And that was it. The show was dead. He had to like it. Even more so, he had to love it. There wasn't much middle with him. I respected and admired that. You knew where the fucking guy stood at all times. He had seen me in the ring once, practicing, and he thought I was moving slow. "Lose fifty pounds," he said without any emotion. And I did it.

By the way, he wanted me to wear red as part of my new character, but I really hate the color red. That was killing me. Snoop and his crew sent a bunch of track suits for me to wear and I compromised by cutting off some of the red sleeves. Snoop was excited for me. That made me feel good.

There's really nothing like waiting to go out through that curtain into the ring. For better or worse, you know what is out there. What was worse for me on that first night was, I was actually running out backwards, so all kinds of shit could have gone wrong. But I was trying not to think about that. I was trying to focus on going out there and on what I was taught. So I went out there that night and I saw that Scott Armstrong was the referee, which was cool. He had always been good to me, and with him in the ring I knew that I was set up for success. This was mine to fuck up. So I got out there, and interestingly, the place was quiet. I could almost hear a pin drop. Then, out of nowhere, this guy who's maybe in his mid-thirties stood up and screamed like a banshee, "You suck, Brodus Clay!" *Well, alright. What the fuck do I do now?* Basically what I had done for my whole life. Try and deflate the situation with a little bit of humor. I looked back over my shoulder, shrugged with a big smile on my face, and said, "My bad!"

The arena broke up, the ice had been broken, and off we went. It was a pretty good match, I won, and everything felt pretty good. I danced around, I did my thing, I got off a lot of good one-liners, and I was no longer the heel that everybody expected me to be. And the girls were amazing. I thought we had done well, but thinking you've done well doesn't mean anything. It's not about what you think. It's about what *they* think. The good news was, there were lots of smiles and back slaps backstage. Everybody seemed relaxed and relieved that I had pulled off this new character. Especially Vince McMahon. That really made my night. He came over, smiled, and said, "Good job." That was good. That was all I needed to hear. When he supports something, gives it his blessing, he doesn't do it lightly. And you know that there is something good going on with your act for him to bless it. And then, my new character took off almost instantly. I was doing all kinds of commercials and promos, fans were going crazy, and the internet was lighting up. Exactly what everybody wanted.

Sadly, I couldn't really enjoy it. Somebody I respected that shall remain nameless came over to me right after the thing started taking off and said, "Wow, I can't even believe you're doing this thing. You should be ashamed yourself." I said, "What the fuck you talking about?" He said to me, "Uncle-Tomming it out there. Nice way for a Brother to make a fool of himself and other Brothers." Now, I knew he was wrong. He had the entire situation wrong. I basically told him to shut the fuck up. But it still bothered me. It still got to me. And it made me realize, with my life at that point, I really couldn't be happy, no matter what was going on. A little comment like that would get me thinking *You don't deserve this. You don't deserve anything good. You're just waiting for the floor to drop out from under you.* My life up until that point had conditioned me to expect a total failure, no matter what was going on. Success was an illusion to me. Even though it seemed real to everybody else because, in actuality, it was real, I just couldn't see it or process it like that. So the irony was, the bigger the character, the more successful it became, the sadder and more removed I became. I know that's hard to imagine, but that's how dysfunctional I was at that time. I'm not going to say there weren't some good moments. Every time I went out in that ring, it was wonderful. You looked at the kids, you looked at families, and you saw the smiles and knew you were making lives better. I loved that. I always will. But you're not out in the ring that often. Most of the time you're in the real world. And for me, that was hell. In the real world, things went wrong for me all the time. That's why I loved the fantasy of being in the ring. It was my safety zone. Nobody could get to me there. But again, that was only a couple of hours a week. Most of the time I was dealing with my own shit, my own fears, and my own bad reactions to things like my response to what that person said to me. I was not in a mentally healthy place, even though I was achieving anything beyond my wildest imaginations. For a kid who was the biggest wrestling fan in his neighborhood and maybe even on the planet—for that kid to become the hero he always dreamed of—there should have been no problems. But life doesn't work that way. We are who we are, no matter what successes or defeats we experience. Funkasaurus was bringing joy to many people, but not to me.

I know that a lot of my feelings were based on my life experiences up until that point. Specific things I had gone through. But it wasn't lost on me, from a racial standpoint, that for many young Black men in America, oftentimes there were feelings of guilt and frustration, even when we did nothing wrong. I'm not going to make it all about that because I don't think race dictates everything in America—I really don't. But I do know the harsh reality and the fact is, being Black is oftentimes a strike against you, and that wears on you. But my unhappiness was mostly about my emotional scars as opposed to the color of my skin.

Despite everything that I was feeling, we still rode that Funkasaurus train as long as we could. But then something happened. We were down in Australia getting ready to do some big shows. Me and the girls were getting ready to appear on the local version of *Good Morning America* when we got a phone call: The powers that be told us that Ariane was being sent home. *What the fuck? Things were blowing up!* I swear that entire continent was fired up, having us there. Why was she being sent back? Turned out, it had to do with previously getting pulled over by a sheriff for suspicion of driving under the influence. She supposedly offered the sheriff a $10,000 bribe to let her go, and it was coming back to haunt her. I knew nothing about it and neither did Naomi. We were both caught totally off guard and didn't know what to do. When we got back home, they took us off television and I was pissed off in a way I had rarely been before. I felt like I was being punished for something I didn't do. I became resentful and hard to deal with. I hated the fact that our trajectory had been thrown off by this one incident. I thought we were bigger than that. I thought we were better than that in the eyes of the powers that be. But nobody was taking any chances. I will say, Ariane handled it far better than I did. She accepted it. She knew what she did was wrong and had no problem with the consequence. But then again, she was the one responsible for the whole mess.

CHAPTER 25

WrestleMania 29

It was getting harder and harder for me to get a match. I was on the road with the WWE, which was great, but I wasn't getting scheduled to do anything and I was getting tired of watching. I'm not a good watcher. The big ego blow for me was when we rolled into Los Angeles for an event at the Staples Center. That's where I wanted to be. In the ring, in that arena in front of the fans and, no doubt, some old friends of mine. I was ready. But my match got cut. I ended up not being on the card. So I got frustrated. I also started getting paranoid. Who didn't want me up there on that stage? Who was working against me? Was it a conspiracy? People secretly conspiring against me? I didn't know, and it didn't feel good.

At that point I was part of the tag team called Tons of Funk, with Matt Bloom aka "Lord Tensai." He was handling it all in stride. He was a pro. I knew at that point he was getting ready to wrap up his wrestling career and move on to becoming a trainer or an agent. He was a veteran wrestler, and he was a lot smarter than me and so he kept his shit together. He just rolled with it because he knew that's how it was. He didn't take everything so personally like I did. Hey, I should have been fine. There were plenty of wrestlers in the world who would have given their left nut to be in my position—which was out there with the show. You never knew when things were going to change for the better. I was busy focusing on the worst. Tensai was cool. Nothing phased him. I just started thinking I was on the way out. I wasn't believing in myself anymore.

At a certain point, nothing else really mattered except what was going to be happening on April 7, 2013, at MetLife stadium in East Rutherford, New Jersey. It was WrestleMania 29, the annual pay-per-view extravaganza produced by WWE. The main event was going to be John Cena versus the Rock. There were a few other prominent matches, including the Undertaker versus CM Punk and Triple H going up against Brock Lesnar. My old partner Alberto del Rio would also be on the card that night, going up against Jack Swagger. There were going to be more than eighty thousand fans in the stadium that night. It would go on to become the WWE's highest-grossing live event, and I knew early it was going to be big night. And when we found out that we were going to be on the card, I stopped bitching and I stopped being paranoid. This was it. This was going to be the single greatest moment of my life. What I had been waiting for. A chance to wrestle at WrestleMania.

I had made appearances at several WrestleManias over the years—dancing, of all things—but I never actually wrestled at one of them. So this would be the single most important thing to me in my life. And so Tensai and I got ready for it—and I mean ready. This wasn't just going to be a chance to appear on the biggest show on earth. It would also be a chance to relaunch myself on a much bigger stage. I also got word weeks before the event that I'd be getting a "pin fault," which meant I would win the match. That was cool.

Tensai and I went all out. As the Tons of Funk, we were going to look more badass than we ever had. We went out and bought ourselves these amazing breakaway pinstripe suits like mobsters. We bought special boots with white cuffs over them for that old-school gangster look. We had everything together. We were going to do this right. This was the fucking moment. We even got some temporary face tattoos. Tons of Funk was going to bring the house down. We were going to make the crowd forget everybody else on that card. At least that was the goal.

Backstage, the mood was quiet and serious. Tensai had been there before, but for me this was the biggest moment of my life. I was all about the game face. About five minutes before curtain, we got in place. When you're behind the curtain, you stand there, waiting for the boss, Vince McMahon himself on headsets, to say, "Go. Get out there." *This is it. The Super Bowl.* But something was wrong. Five minutes went by and Undertaker was still out there with CM Punk. *What the fuck? What the actual fuck?* We were one minute late getting to the ring. Then two minutes late. Then three minutes late. I could hear the match out there; they would get to one count and two count, but before the match would be over, they just extended their routine. What the hell were they doing? They didn't need an extra ten minutes. They had been in the spotlight many times. I was standing against that piece of fabric thinking that that was the only thing standing between me and immortality—that fucking curtain. And I knew what was going to happen. Undertaker and CM Punk were going over five or ten minutes, and that meant we were going to get cut. Or at least that was the fear. Was that really going to happen this time? Was that really how my dreams were going to come crashing down?

I held out hope against hope, but then I knew it was over. Vince McMahon stood up, took his headphones, and said, "I did everything I could, Brodus. I'm sorry."

"It's okay, boss," I said to him. "It's okay." But it wasn't okay. When I realized that the dream was over, I turned around and walked out of the stadium. I literally walked out of the parking lot. I thought I looked so cool ten minutes earlier. Now I was just a big asshole in a pinstripe suit with nowhere to go. I wandered out in the parking lot. I could hear what was happening inside—eighty thousand people going crazy. I looked like a pimp with no girls around me. After a while I tried to get back into the building.

The security guy said to me, "Do you have a pass?"

"Fucking look at me," I said.

"Brodus! What are you doing out here?"

"They cut my match."

"Those motherfuckers. I am so sorry."

I explained that I had left my keys inside and had to go get the rest of my stuff, so he let me in. They say "chase your dreams," but they never say "read the fine print." My dream had come to an end. And that was all she wrote.

I felt humiliated as I went to collect my stuff. I couldn't get out of the building fast enough. Back at the hotel, I tweeted, "You never know how much you love something until it breaks your heart. The good news is you know you love something that much. I'll be back. 365 till redemption." Then I went to bed.

The next morning in the hotel lobby, Linda McMahon saw me. She came over and said, "Listen, I'm so sorry your match got cut. It's a real shame. But I saw what you posted last night and I love that thought. You have to have faith in yourself. It's going to be okay." She was so classy and I really appreciated her words. I genuinely believe both she and Vince knew how hard this was for me.

Getting my match cut was a bitter pill for me to swallow. I didn't know what was next. But this was going take a long time to get over.

CHAPTER 26

Impact (2014)

I was driving to work out at Hard Knock South on a Wednesday morning when I got a call from Mark Carrano, the head of talent at WWE. He was the guy who would call you if you were booked on a commercial or something. He was also the guy who would call you if you were getting canned. When he called, you knew he could either make your day or ruin your day, and he seemed to have the same tone whether he was delivering good news or bad. As soon as I heard his voice, I could tell it was not good news. He couldn't hide it.

"I don't know what happened," he said. "We were on a rocket ship on the way to the top and all of a sudden, the wheels just came off. I hate to tell you this, but we are releasing you."

I took the news without much emotion. I had not been working all that much at that point so there wasn't really good money for me in it.

"Look, never say never," Mark said. "You made it back once before and it could happen again. There is definitely something about you. But right now I'm sorry to say that we just have to part ways. We appreciate all you did for the WWE and we wish you the best of luck in the future."

I called my trainer from the car and told him the news. He wanted to know if I was going to skip my workout and I said, "Nope. I'll be there. Just letting you know." Maybe I was in shock, but I was just rolling with it. I had a good workout, went about my day, and a few hours later when I got home, I realized that I had missed about twenty-five calls from a variety of wrestling promoters all trying to book me.

I wasn't in the mood to respond to any of them. I guess I was still processing getting fired. It sucks when you get fired. Many times, people want to talk shit about the place that cut them loose, but that's not me. I love the WWE. No way I was going to say anything bad about them. I don't think I would ever bash a former employer even if I didn't like them. I just don't think it's right. But evidently, the news of them letting me go had hit the internet and the calls kept rolling in. Still, I was taking the day off, not responding to anyone.

The next day I was driving home from working out when I got a phone call from an unknown number. For some reason, I answered. It was a guy from Impact wrestling. This was interesting to me. Impact was basically the number two in the business behind WWE and they were a great company. Dixie Carter was helping to run the show, and I really respected her. This guy asked me, "When are your ninety days up?" See, in the WWE, when they let you go, they basically pay you three months' severance. It's a classy move. The only stipulation is that you can't work for anybody that involves wrestling on television. Not a big deal. So I basically took out a calendar and counted off the days. He said to me, "Okay, on the nine-tieth day we would love to have you here." I accepted the invitation. We would work out the details later, but it felt like the right move. I had been unemployed for only a couple of days and then there I was at Impact. Eventually, Dixie made a very generous offer and I was excited once we started up. I knew it was the right decision.

At Impact, you could tell wrestlers had a lot more freedom. It was less scripted. That made me comfortable. I also knew a lot of the guys there and had worked with many of them over the years. I'll admit, the first few months were a bit tough because you were going through what I call "WWE shock." How the WWE did things was just ingrained in your mind. Don't get me wrong, I love how the WWE does things. It's just different than Impact. What I began learning at Impact was that things were more spontaneous and had fewer restraints. You didn't have to ask permission to try things. It was more about *you* as opposed to the brand. That meant it was a much less pressure-packed situation. You weren't worried about screwing up because pretty much anything went. WWE focuses a lot on camera angles and entrances and the drama of the spectacle. That works for them because that's their brand. Impact was scrappier and looser. It felt like a great new home for me then and still does today.

CHAPTER 27

Meeting Gutfeld (2014)

By that point, I had been wrestling under the name of "Tyrus" and the personality had begun to grow. It was getting popular. I was busy painting my career canvas, and then something called Fox News spilled an entirely new and different kind of paint right at my feet.

It started out simply enough. This guy on Fox News I didn't know much about, Greg Gutfeld, had made some joke on Twitter. I can't even remember what it was. Like I said, I hadn't seen much of him. I think I had watched his show, *Red Eye*, a couple of times, and maybe saw a couple of minutes of the *Greg Gutfeld Show* in an airport or something. That was it. So he made a joke; I guess it cracked me up and I retweeted it. That was it.

Literally just a few minutes later, I got a private message from him inviting me up to New York to appear on his show. It struck me as a little bit weird at first. Here was this little white guy who wanted to goof on the big wrestler guy. That was how it seemed to me. That was a serious red flag. I didn't take his invitation seriously at all. But then one of his producers contacted me with flight information to New York. Okay, so it was the real deal. I would give it a shot.

As of this writing, the *Greg Gutfeld Show* is a very big deal. A massive success. Back then it was still pretty new. There wasn't even a studio audience. We had some fun right at the beginning. I literally carried him out onto the set. I don't think the other cohosts were too crazy about me being there. People automatically look down their noses at pro wrestlers. They think we are all the same. But I hung in there and got off a couple of good lines. I remember the first question had to do with Ariana Grande. There had just been a TMZ video released of her taking a bite from a donut at some store and then putting it back and making an anti-American crack after she got busted. I went off on that a little bit, and right into the first commercial break, Greg leaned over and whispered to me, "If you lived in New York, I would make you a cohost. You're terrific."

Well, that was interesting. I couldn't move to New York then—I was busy with everything else—but I said to him, "What if maybe we did once a month or so?" He said, "I'll take it." That was the beginning. I knew it wasn't going to be a huge money gig right out of the gate, but I did think that it would be a smart way to rebrand myself, bring out some more humor, and even become a little bit more serious when it came to discussing social issues. Within a few short months I had become a regular on the show.

Impact was having its problems. As great as Dixie Carter was, it was still tough. Pro wrestling is such a cutthroat business. I was always paid, even if sometimes the checks were a little bit late. But I'm not sure about everybody else there. I know there were some guys on the crew and behind the scenes that sometimes waited a long time for their checks to clear. Impact just didn't have the budget to get everything done the way it needed to be done. WWE is totally different. They have resources and they can probably go on forever, but for Impact it was a totally different situation. Meanwhile, though, over at Fox News, things were going well and getting busier.

I began flying up there once a week and all of a sudden Greg was campaigning Fox to give me a contract. It was very flattering. A lot of the things I was talking about started to go viral. Just a comment here or there in most cases, but sometimes a full-on rant. Wherever my head and my heart were that day, I would just spit out my thoughts and feelings, and sometimes my opinions and observations caught fire. Everybody at Fox liked that because it translated into higher ratings. I think part of the reason I was starting to thrive at Fox was the fact that I brought an entirely different perspective than everybody else they had there. Yes, I have been pulled over by some of the nicest cops you would ever want to meet. But I also had been fucked over by some of the worst scumbags on the planet. I will say that throughout my life, 90 to 95 percent of my interactions with cops have been quite positive. I always hold individuals accountable as well, not an entire department. Unless of course there's something systemic and/or rotten from the top down. You never know that when you get pulled over; all you know is who you're dealing with. Every business has bad apples. And I wouldn't be surprised if, like my experiences with cops, it shook out to about 95 percent good people to 5 percent assholes wherever you go. That's just the way life is.

As word spread to the other shows at Fox, all of a sudden, I was getting invites. I remember the first time I did *The Five*.

That blew my mind. I had seen the show before, I liked it, but I could never picture myself on that panel. Part of me didn't feel like I was part of the Fox world. I didn't look like most of them, I didn't talk like most of them, and I didn't live like most of them. I had voted twice for Barack Obama, yet in my heart I considered myself a small-government Republican. I was all over the map politically, which definitely didn't fit the stereotype of a Fox News personality. But I was finding my voice at Fox and everybody was very supportive of that process. I knew about all the Fox News stereotypes. I knew that supposedly it was a bunch of good old conservative white boys having their way with everybody. But as I learned, that oversimplification was just a lot of bullshit. To believe many people, Fox News is nothing more than a bunch of suit-wearing white nationalists. And if they had Brothers on the air, well, then, those are not really Brothers—those were people with Black skin who thought less of Black people than white people did. That's what everybody said.

I remember the first time I met Sean Hannity. I was ready to hate the guy, only because of what I had read about him before I started working at Fox. Well, guess what? He could not have been any nicer to me. He listened to me, and he told me that his door was always open in case I needed anything. He goofed a little bit on my tattoos, but that was Sean. That was just him keeping it real. He certainly was not the fire-breathing racist that so many other "journalists" would have had you believe. He was just a stand-up guy who looked you in the eye and talked to you and gave you a real handshake like he meant it.

I was fearful of Judge Jeanine Pirro because I thought she was going to be a tyrant. She just comes across as tough as nails. I avoided her at any cost. Then one day I was walking down the hallway and I heard her voice. "Tyrus, come over here!" In my head, I was thinking, *Where's my ID? I don't have any warrants....* I mean, she was all about law and order...right? So how could I not be thinking like that? Well, just like Hannity, she was one of the nicest people I'd ever met. She invited me on her show, wanted to make sure everything was going well at Fox, and also extended herself to me if I needed anything at all. I started thinking to myself, *I need to start looking at how I look at people. I don't want to be prejudged, and these people are not white devils.* They all went out of their way to make me feel comfortable, and I noticed a ton of multiculturalism when it came to both cast and crew. Look, I'm not stupid. Every business has its problems and so does Fox. No place is perfect. But guess what? Companies deal with those things and move on. You don't get to be the number one cable news network by being a hotbed of racism and sexism. Fox has dealt with problems as best they can, with discretion and justice. Every place has its challenges. And when you're Fox News and have most of the free world gunning for you, everything is going to be exaggerated. I can tell you personally, Fox News is the single most inclusive, tolerant, and fair place I have ever worked.

But when it came to all the personalities there, one person who stood out at the beginning still stands out today: Dana Perino. I'm not even sure how to best describe her. She is simply the most professional, intelligent person I have ever worked with and may even be the most professional, intelligent person I have ever met. From the moment I met her she was gracious, classy, kind, and as giving as anybody could have been. She gave me advice, she supported me, she had me on her shows, and she was always there to answer any question I ever had. She is so accomplished and has had such a distinguished career that I feel really blessed that I'm able to work with her. That kind of television was entirely new to me. I never went to school for it. I didn't know how to play. Dana has given me so much advice and consultation over the years that I can't even think of how I might thank her. And whenever I hear people criticizing Fox News and talking about what a dangerous and destructive place it is, I think of Dana Perino. I defy anybody on this planet to meet her, talk to her, and get to know her, and not come away feeling like I do. For me, she defines Fox News, and I cherish her friendship as much as anything else.

CHAPTER 28

Fox News

When I first arrived at Fox News, I felt totally out of place. For starters, I didn't look like anybody else there. I was a professional wrestler. I didn't wear suits. I had no journalism background. It was intimidating. I was surrounded by people who were polished, educated, and ambitious within the broadcast field. Very talented, and very competitive. The competitive part I was totally down with. But this was not the playing field I was used to. Big, fancy offices, lots of office politics that you could sense around every corner, and a corporate vibe that I had never been exposed to. But I was totally up for the challenge.

As it turned out, I was going to go through a quick baptism by fire. Around my fifth show appearance or so, I saw a serious topic on the rundown sheet that we would get before going on air. We were going to be talking about a recent spate of resisting arrest cases, and there was a video that supposedly showed police brutality against Black men. It was becoming part of the national conversation at warp speed, which is why it was going to be tackled on the show. Here's the thing: I was not a serious news or social analyst. I was the big, dumb wrestler, there to crack jokes and say pretty much anything that kept things lively, humorous, and a bit irreverent. I was not the go-to guy for serious issues. It wasn't my role. Now, we had a guy in St. Louis who had been choked out by a cop, and a number of other cases that did not look good for the police. So I flew up to New York City, visited my buddy Joe at his apartment to play video games with some free time I had, opened up that rundown sheet on my phone, and saw what was coming up on that episode. I started getting scared.

I didn't know what the fuck I was going to say when they got to me on the panel. Over the course of my life, I've been on the ground with a cop's gun at my forehead, I've been zip-tied, and I've been accused of having drugs on me and stealing cars—things I had nothing to do with. But I've also had some great experiences with cops. The more I thought about it, the more nervous I became, imagining how that episode was going to go down. Watching how people on social media had started mobilizing against things that they didn't agree with, the first wave of what became known as "cancel culture," I began to imagine what would happen if I sided with the cops: "He's an Uncle Tom!" Or if I took the side of the victim: "He's a BLM extremist!" At that moment, there were movies I was interested in auditioning for, and other career opportunities beyond Fox. I could easily see all those things disappearing, depending on how the segment would shake out. For other commentators on Fox, it was no big deal. People knew where they stood politically, so nothing would be shocking. I was new to this game, and I didn't want to fuck up all of the other opportunities that were starting to emerge on the horizon.

While I was sitting in Joe's apartment, I expressed to him my fears and concerns after reading the sheet. "Hey," I asked him. "You have cop friends, right?" I was aware that over the years he had become connected with a number of New York City police officers. Right away, he pulled out a few phone numbers and said, "Call these guys right now. I think they can help you get through this and shape an opinion that's true to yourself."

The first guy I got on the phone was blunt with me. "Obviously there are bad cops out there. Every profession has bad people in it. But for a lot of us, it's gotten even harder out there on the streets. People pull out their cameras after things start going wrong, and that's what gets posted on social media. But rarely do they record what got us to that critical point. The one thing we stress over and over to people is that they need to comply with what we ask them to do. Compliance is key. If we are arresting you, that's not the time to be a martyr." That made total sense to me. I called another of Joe's friends, and he reiterated those same points. He also added that in today's age with all this technology, bad cops usually get recognized right away. I hung up the phone, sat back, and started thinking. Then it was time to go to the show and get ready.

As usual, I kept to myself while everybody else was in makeup. Then, we were on the set, the red lights went on, and we were off and running. I was feeling the butterflies when Greg steered the conversation toward this highly sensitive topic. The word I needed to remember was "compliant" because that, for me, really was the key to all of this.

"Tyrus, what do you think of all of this?" Greg finally said. I took a deep breath and then I started my answer, telling the viewers basically, if I get pulled over, then that's a bad day.

I'm a big Black guy. Six foot, eight inches. All tatted up. And if it's a bad cop? That really sucks. Because he's going to win every time. And all I'm going to want at that moment is to go home. And if you have done something wrong or if there's a warrant for you, well, guess what, you are going to jail. At that moment, you need to comply. If that cop is screwing you over, because of body cams and everything today, don't worry, you will get lawyers and they will make you rich once all is said and done. If you are in the wrong, that's a whole different story. You are going to lose every time. Regardless, either way, that is the law, and when they tell you to comply, you comply. That's where I took the topic before adding, "If you choose to resist arrest, that doesn't make you Rosa Parks. That makes you a criminal."

All hell broke loose. That single sentence about Rosa Parks went viral. Once the show aired, I started getting hundreds of messages—including dozens from cops all over the country, writing to thank me. In that segment, I talked about the fact that there are bad cops out there. The cops writing me were thanking me for being so honest because they were aware of it as well. Obviously, the fact that I had been on both sides of the issue really affected people and helped my words become relatable to a much larger audience than had I simply come down on one side. I was speaking from the heart; I was speaking my truth, and it was resonating with people. That became the most-watched segment ever on the show. Greg came to me and said, "I need you every week. We need what you bring."

I had been so nervous about that moment and, as it turned out, it became the moment that helped launch me in the eyes of many. I think the executives at Fox appreciated it because I was bringing balance to an issue based on real-life experience. Nobody else on that panel had been dragged out of a car with a cop barking, "Where are your drugs, man?" From that point on, simply for speaking my truth, the audience reacted and related differently to me. When I was out on the street in New York, people started coming over to me, talking about that segment, telling me how much they appreciated the fact that I was being honest and making strong points. I mean, come on, it's common sense, right? Well, you know what they say about common sense these days: it's not that common anymore.

Leading up to the 2016 presidential election, as many of you I'm sure remember, lots of shit hit the fan in that last month. Leading up to November you had Hillary's health issues, email investigations, her "deplorable" comments, and many other missteps that she made. But Trump also had a lot of serious baggage, not the least of which was a video in which he could be heard talking about grabbing women by their pussies. He introduced that phrase to the American lexicon. "Grab her by the pussy!" I was disgusted with both of them. I was frustrated because I know how important it is to vote, but neither of these two motherfuckers did anything for me. Just being honest. As I was about to learn, sometimes honesty can also get you in some trouble. On one of our shows leading up to the election, Greg asked me who I was going to vote for. I was blunt. That's what they were paying me for, in my mind. I let it out. I said, "I think we have two bad choices and, like a lot of Americans, I don't feel good either way. So you know what? I'm done. I'm probably not going to even vote, and if I do, I may just put John McCain's name in there as a protest."

Part of me was joking and part of me was serious. That's where my head was. I got back in the green room after the show and nobody was talking to me. In fact, I sort of detected some chilliness from the producer. Oh well, whatever. I flew back home, back to my life down south. As the week progressed, I noticed that no plans had been made for my flight back to New York to do the show at the end of the next week. That was weird. Usually, somebody would call and ask me where I wanted to fly out of and into, depending on what else was going on in my life. But nobody had checked up on my travel. I called my producer to ask what was going on and she said to me, "Tyrus, we're going to take a break with you. You told the nation you're not voting, and that's not really the message we want to get out there. Given your position, I think for the next week we're just going to go in another direction."

Wait a minute. I was being benched for making a joke? I tried pressing the issue, but she was adamant. "We're going to have somebody on the show who is going to be more positive when it comes to the voting process. You'll be back. But we value the election process and don't want to be in the business of promoting the idea of not going to the polls."

That sucked. I was confused. I was frustrated. I thought the whole point of having me on was for me to speak my mind. But there was definitely a lesson happening right in front of my eyes. It was my time to realize that there was a responsibility to your words, and that sometimes there was also a consequence. My bosses perceived me as being irresponsible. Look, it's their playground, not mine. It definitely hurt to get pulled out of the lineup. I'm still not sure what they did was totally fair, but they write the checks. I respect and understand that today, but back in 2016 I was pissed off—so much so that I just had the urge to get away. I decided a little vacation was in order, so I hopped a flight to the Cayman Islands to get some distance and clear my head.

Come election night, I was sitting in my little cabana, waiting for the returns to start coming in, but I didn't like watching all of this alone because it started getting kind of exciting once it became clear the election was not going to be a slam dunk for Hillary Clinton. I wandered over to the small bar that was part of the hotel where I was staying. A bunch of folks had gathered to watch the election returns, and, as I was walking in, someone jumped out of the bushes by the entranceway and scared the living shit out of me. "Tyrus," the guy barked, "What the hell are you doing here?" I was staring right in the eyes of Robert O'Neill, the guy who killed Osama bin Laden.

"Dude," I laughed. "Is this how Fox News deals with somebody who talks out of line? They send an assassin to the Cayman Islands to take care of business?" We had a good laugh. He and I knew each other from appearing on numerous shows together at Fox, and although he definitely startled me, it was also pretty funny. I liked and respected him. The little commotion we caused attracted the attention of many people in the bar, and then one after another they started coming up to me. I mean, who knew there were so many Fox News fans in the Cayman Islands? "Why aren't you on TV tonight?" somebody wanted to know. I explained what had happened. "We saw what you said. It wasn't a big deal!" It was cool having so much support in that little tropical tavern, and it made me feel better about the whole incident.

Little by little it became evident that not only was Hillary not a lock to win, but that things were slipping away right before everybody's eyes. Going to bed that night, I wondered what it would be like up at Fox News with Trump as president. Would we all still be able to speak our minds? Would any new rules be set in place?

As far as Trump winning, I can't say I was that surprised or shocked. Throughout the entire campaign, I had found Hillary arrogant, overconfident, and very self-entitled. As it turned out, it was women who decided the election when they, in large numbers, rejected Hillary. Women were not voting by gender. Hillary had counted on that and needed that to win. Also, I felt like she felt she deserved to win, as opposed to Trump, who acted like he truly wanted to win. That's a big difference.

My attitude with presidents has always been, it's really not about the Oval Office. It's about the Senate Chamber. That's where the shit goes on. That's the place that decides what's happening in our country. The mess we're living in right now as you read this in real time, for me, goes back to when Mitch McConnell and his band of thieves decided they were going to "Make Barack Obama a one-term president." That's when this mess really started—the extreme partisan politics, the all-around toxicity that defines today's political climate. That set up the payback once Trump took office. Personally, I think it's time for term limits in the Senate. They get too comfortable up there, getting all connected, and I think it's hurting our country. There's no other job that lets you stay there forever, as long as you can get elected. And the longer you stay there, the better your chances become because the deeper your connections become. So even though people on the Left were freaking out about Donald Trump, in my head it was never really going to be about Trump. It was going to be about the Senators.

Also, sure enough, the Democrats decided early in the game that Trump needed to be impeached. No evidence, nothing to hang him with, but it didn't matter. After what Mitch McConnell had started, it was game on—and they played well. Trump never had one easy day in office when it came to Democrats.

As far as Trump himself, I had plenty of issues with him and spoke about them frequently on air. I have to admit, though, I did like how, right out of the gate, Trump called everybody out, even Republicans, who quickly fell in line for the most part for fear of him. I wasn't crazy about his Twitter presence, although it did help keep regular Americans plugged in to the system. But with the way Trump was with Twitter, to me, it was like two elephants having sex in your yard. For the first couple of days, it's an incredible thing to witness. You invite your friends over. Your neighbors come over. It's a fucking spectacle. But after about a week it starts getting old. "Yo, can you move your trunk so I can get to my front door? Get a fucking room already!" That's the way I felt about Trump on Twitter. Super entertaining at first, but it got old very fast.

Trump was obviously a big part of our show. He was a big part of every show on every network. There's never been a president that was as good for the media as Donald Trump. Viewership went up across the board because of the battles that were happening between Trump and certain specific reporters, like Jim Acosta. Trump's battle with the media became the game within the game; it was entertaining, it was reality TV, it was pro wrestling, it was good versus evil. Of course, whichever side you were on determined which was good and which was evil.

CHAPTER 29

Trump

During the campaign, Greg Gutfeld had been very critical of Trump. But once Trump became president, I think Greg began to relate to him a little bit, because, like Trump, Greg has always been a disruptor himself. He's always been challenging people, always speaking out and exposing hypocrisy, corruption, and the like, so although they had different ways of going about it, I do think that Greg came to realize that he and Trump had similar goals. It was all about blowing things fucking wide open and bringing the establishment to its knees. I respect that in both of those guys because whatever you think of them, they walk it like they talk it. They're not afraid to upset the status quo. In fact, they're afraid of not upsetting the status quo. That takes plenty of guts and plenty of balls, and the headaches that come from taking those stances are hard to describe to those who don't know what it's like on the inside. People like that deal with a lot of shit behind the scenes and yet they still get out there every day, put on the gloves, and let people have it.

Our show definitely benefited from Trump being president, and not just because we have a large Republican viewer base. A lot of moderate Democrats were also tuning in to us because we also occasionally made fun of Trump when he earned it. That's the thing. We were far more honest about him, in my opinion, than any of the other networks. On our show, if Trump tweeted something stupid, we talked about it. Our audience went from about four hundred thousand to one million to two million—and just kept exploding after that. I was always recognized on the streets because of my wrestling and at that point, more than ever before, people were going crazy; I had little old white ladies running towards me, whereas not long before they would have been running away from me. Everywhere I went people would come up to me and replay bits from the show: their favorite jokes, their favorite takes, telling me how much they loved Trump but also how much they hated Trump. I heard from everybody and I just loved it. What that said to me was that we were resonating with lots of different kinds of people. The bigger our audience group, the more I came to realize it really wasn't a good idea to say I wasn't going to vote. I started realizing that my words had meaning and gravity. If a hundred people didn't vote because I said something about it, that's nothing I would be proud of. I always try and stay open to learning lessons, even when I disagree with the original premise.

While I was proud of how our show, for the most part, dealt with Trump, I was embarrassed for reporters like Jim Acosta who became household names by tangling with Trump. I'm not a journalist by trade, but one thing I did learn early was that it's never a good idea to become part of the story. And on Greg's show, none of us did. We stuck to the facts, we gave our opinions, and we tried to find some humor in a lot of the craziness, but we never became part of the story.

Barack Obama had changed my soul, but Donald Trump changed my mind. What I mean by that is, when Obama was elected, I cried. I voted for him twice and it really meant a lot to me to have a Black man in the White House. Was he perfect? Of course not. But he changed my soul. He made me believe in things that I thought were never possible. Now, when I say that Trump changed my mind, he affected the way I think. I like how important it was for Trump to expose the system for the common man. When he gave speeches and when he dealt with the press, he was very deliberate about putting information out there; for the most part, it gave voters a chance to really understand how ugly the back of the political kitchen was. I know that he also embellished things from time to time and in some cases may have flat-out lied, but that wasn't the majority of what he said, at least not in my view. Up until the pandemic, you have to remember, Trump was a popular president. The economy was roaring like gangbusters and many of his proposals had resulted in very positive things for the country. But in the end, I believe it was the pandemic that did him in. No president is prepared for something that catastrophic.

That being said, he still could not control himself and went off script too many times, relying more on his bravado and self-importance than the knowledge of scientists and others around him. He wanted everything to end so quickly that he oversimplified and gave people a false sense of security of when things might be better. Obviously, that didn't work.

One thing, though, that really did piss me off about Trump was his position on kneeling in the NFL. As I discussed numerous times on the air, I completely disagreed with Trump's attitude toward NFL players. When he would go after guys and start making the whole issue about being "patriotic," that made me nuts. I could not have disagreed more with him. Nobody at Fox ever had a problem with me voicing that opinion. That's why I love working at Fox. People's perceptions about the network, I think, have always been wrong, but they never became more inaccurate than after Trump was elected. Critics would say "It's an all-white network" and things like that. Until you go in the building and work in the building and hang out with people in the building, you have no idea how diverse that network is. People from all walks of life, from every ethnicity, they are all there every day. What's more, Fox allows me to be who I am, wearing my backward baseball caps, T shirts, and such; they let me do my thing and I don't think any other network would do that. Think of it. CNN, MSNBC—is there anybody else like me on any of those networks? The more I learn and the more I grow as a commentator and a contributor, the more I respect what goes on at Fox News. They gave me a shot; they invited me into their house knowing very little about me. Rough as I am, they accept me and encourage me to be myself. That tells you a lot right there.

CHAPTER 30

Closing Thoughts

Well, you made it this far with me. For that, I owe you a big thanks and a ton of gratitude. I know I'm not the easiest guy to get along with. I realize some of the stories may have upset you, but in the end, I hope you at least sense that I'm real. If nothing else, I'm real. That's truly why I wrote this book. I wanted people to get to know me—the good, the bad, and the ugly. I know there is lots of ugly, but I like to believe that today, there is just as much good. My main takeaway from this experience of just putting my life down on paper is that if nothing else, I always learn to be accountable for myself because I never had an outlet to blame anyone else. I wasn't raised by anybody who taught me lessons on a regular basis. I have had some good mentors for sure, but in terms of those critical early years, I pretty much raised myself. When you do that, you learn about accountability pretty fast.

As an adult, and as a parent today, one of the things I preach to my kids is that no matter how people may come after you and attack you, it's your reaction that defines you. You can't allow yourself to become a slave to their emotions and reactions. And today, there will always be people coming after you, especially if you decide to use your voice and fight for what you believe in. Growing up, I was called fat, I was called ugly, I was called all kinds of horrible names because of the color my skin, and I had to learn to measure my reactions. It took a long time, but I'm finally there. I also learned that when people attack you, it means that they are either scared of you or jealous of you. They are acting out on something that they are scared to confront. That's why you can't let their attacks turn you into something that you're not. I know it sounds like I'm oversimplifying and hell, maybe I am, I do that a lot, but I really believe that the expression, "Sticks and stones may break my bones but words can never hurt me" really is a mantra to live by. It's not how big you are; it's how tough inside you are. I'm a big guy. I get it. I've been in lots of fights. But at the end of the day, as a grown man today, I will not let words hurt me. Come after me physically, come after my family, we will have another conversation. But there's nothing you can say to me that will throw me off my course or life path. Words are just words. I wish more people realized that.

Looking back on my life, I think the three most influential figures to me—at least as a young person—were the Incredible Hulk, Jimmie "JJ" Walker in *Good Times*, and, of course, Dusty Rhodes, the American Dream. For me, these three bigger-than-life characters combined represented courage, loyalty, trust, humor, and a no-bullshit attitude when it comes to standing up for yourself. Early on, I was definitely guilty of taking the lazy way out and blaming others when I would fall short. When I finally learned to be accountable for myself, that's when I truly became a man. That's when I became someone that my kids today can look up to and be proud of. Social media makes it hard today for many people on the planet. It can cause pressure, anxiety, and trauma, especially when people come after you for whatever reason. Keyboard warriors hide behind anonymous names and do nothing but sit and troll all day. It can be frustrating, but you can't let that wear you down. Never give in to a bully. Empower yourself. Believe in yourself. Be accountable. Life is too short to worry about with the other person is doing. Own your shit. Use your voice. And be kind to others. That's all I got. And I really do sincerely thank you for reading my words.

Some Random Thoughts I've Had About Race, Life, and Politics

Limiting Senate Terms

"We are only given a certain amount of time to do what we were sent here to do. You don't have to be around a long time to share the wisdom of a lifetime. You just have to use your time wisely, efficiently. There is no time to waste."

—MAMIE TILL BRADLEY

The United States Senate unanimously passed recognizing lynching as a federal crime in 2018. I bet Emmett Till is relieved. Emmett Louis Till was a young African-American from Chicago who grew up with segregation and racism, even in Chicago, a fourteen-year-old who, like most young boys, was known to play pranks. Despite him being an honor-roll student and well-behaved child, his mother was not unaware of his prankster-like mentality. Before leaving to visit family in Mississippi, she warned him not to goof around, and that there was an enhanced level of segregation and racism there that he had never experienced before.

While visiting Mississippi, Emmett Till was murdered and became a victim of lynching. He was brutalized and murdered on August 28, 1955, for the color of his skin. The "crime" was allegedly flirting with a white woman four days prior to his murder, where at a local store he was bragging to his cousins that back home in Chicago he had a white girlfriend. His cousins dared him to flirt with the white woman working behind the counter where he was about to purchase candy. Being a jokester, he accepted the dare, and, after he purchased candy, said "Bye, baby" to the woman while walking out of the store.

The woman told her husband, who owned the store, and her brother. The men assembled and drove to the home of Emmett Till's uncle, where they threw the fourteen-year-old boy into their car and proceeded to brutally torture him for hours, lynching the child as punishment for his "crime" of flirting with a white woman. They forced young Emmett Till to carry a seventy-five-pound cotton gin fan to the banks of a river and take off his clothes, then brutalized and beat him nearly to death, gouging his eye out before finally shooting him in the head. They then tied his broken body to the fan using barbed wire and threw his body in the river. His body was discovered three days later and was so disfigured the only way his family identified him was by a ring he wore that had his initials engraved into it.

The local police and authorities wanted to bury his body quickly and pressured his family to do so. His mother, Mamie Till Bradley, refused and demanded the body be transported back to Chicago. His mother saw Emmett's innocent, young, broken, and brutalized body and demanded the world see it, too. She wanted the world to know what happened to him and what racist, hate-filled murderers had done to her only son. She held an open-casket funeral. An African-American magazine picked up the story and published a photo of Emmett Till's corpse. This got the attention of the major media outlets and let the world, in fact, know of what happened to Emmett Till in Mississippi.

As a result, the perpetrators were charged with his murder and stood trial that September in a segregated courthouse in Mississippi. On September 23, 1955, despite multiple witnesses to the identity of his murderers, an all-white jury returned a verdict of "not guilty" after deliberating for less than an hour. The jury stated the "not guilty" verdict was reached not because the defendants' identities weren't proved, but instead because the state had failed to prove that the body was properly identified as Emmett Till. Despite widespread outrage, the state was satisfied and chose not to pursue the additional indictments of kidnapping, and the murderers were set free.

As a result of his mother's determination that the country see and know of Emmett Till's lynching murder, the brutal reality of the Jim Crow segregation in the South was revealed to the country as a whole. The widespread outrage following the trial and the jury's verdict is often credited as sparking the national discussion of racial segregation and the beginning of the Civil Rights movement.

If you are introducing and passing a bill to amend Title 18 of the United States Code to "specify lynching as a depravation of civil rights" and make it a federal crime and name it "Justice for Victims of Lynching Act of 2018," there should be some semblance of genuine care taken with such an overdue, easily passed, common-sense law. If you're not going to give the families of the victims some kind of reparations, it would be actually thoughtful to give some acknowledgment of the pain that this kind of crime causes victims. At the very least, *one* of the senators who wrote the bill, named the bill, cosponsored the bill, or even offered slight amendments (all of which were accepted unanimously) could have reminded themselves that they are supposed to represent *the people* and maybe consider those people they claim to represent by naming the bill after an actual victim like Emmett Till. While he wasn't lynched by hanging, as not all victims of lynching were hanged, he was lynched for the crime of being Black. Or name the bill after his mother, Mamie Till Bradley, who, even in her grief, was strong in her resolve to ensure the country grieve too by forcing America to see and know the reality of Jim Crow and whose actions sparked a national debate that evolved into the Civil Rights movement.

However, instead of recognizing an ugly moment in our history and making it about a historical moment to recognize an American family wronged by the government, denied justice in our court system, and ignored by the justice department, the bill became a feather in the cap of the senators like Sen. Cory Booker, who want America to know *they* are the star. To be fair, this didn't have to be about Emmett or any one person, but encompassing and acknowledging victims would be a great gesture. In my opinion, the politicians who are supposed to work for us and are paid by our tax dollars decided to make a law by proposing and passing a sterilely named bill in a deeply impersonal manner—one that would federally recognize a hate crime that is already illegal in nature. Yet, just because of the fucked-up nature of the crime of lynching and the history of hate behind the specific offense, why not make it about those who suffered? Not politicians elected to represent "we the people" using a horrible crime as a platform and a chip to be played later to cover up laziness and failure to engage on actual issues affecting us now. If the Senate was focused on what's best for the people of the United States, there would be more unanimous votes and less obstructionist bullshit on both sides. Ideology is no excuse for not focusing on working for and with the people who pay you to represent them, despite their politics—people who you are supposed to be fighting for.

This is one example of how bipartisanship does work—just when there's nothing to lose from it. Lynching, like any other assault or homicide, is illegal by itself, so it's redundant in some ways—but it's a long overdue gesture by our representatives to federally recognize lynchings and formally denounce officials and individuals who sanction this action. My point is, we know politicians can only work together, out from their tribe tents, when there's no real risk and only reward for individual egos. Sen. Booker, whom I have a lot of respect for (despite that he couldn't agree on a meal at dinner) has championed this bill. Look, lynching is bad, we know it's bad, and you are going to jail for life if you are a part of it. The cosmetic attempt to get something done for optics and future use on a stump speech to get votes, to just stand on your soapbox and say, "I spearheaded the fight to criminalize lynch mobs!" is bullshit! Now if Sen. Booker added that the families of victims of lynch mobs are to be given reparations for their losses, would the tents close? That would be a risk, and I'm sure it would receive more of the same obstruction bullshit we see now.

The bottom line is that when there is nothing to lose and agreement is obvious, that is when both sides decide to get together and actually work together. Outside of the clear issues, our taxes pay people to throw on their team's jersey and focus on working against each other in order to fight the other side and "win" instead of fighting for the people who pay their salaries, the people they are supposed to represent. We have reached a point where government is a team sport and all that matters is winning: not winning for the people, but winning for whatever side of the aisle that representative sits on.

If there was ever a time for term limits in the Senate, the time it is now. The issue we have in this country right now is that no one is "changing minds." Minds are not being changed, not on anything, and I don't think this closed-mindedness is anything other than a problem with those who represent us. The fact is, whether you're a Republican or a Democrat... enough. In the Senate we repeatedly have 51 to 50 votes, with all Democrats on one side, all Republicans on the other. They forget that just voting on their party's side of an issue is not what they were elected for, and reelected for, and re-reelected for, and so on. Their job is to get the best deal for the American people, not do their own thing, and all we are seeing is a lack of willingness to compromise or join the other side. There is not any example set to show acts of good faith between the sides of the aisle, no meeting halfway. That is what compromise is; when compromise happens, both sides win some and both sides lose some. Instead, both sides are so focused on winning everything and making no concessions that it is not helping and, in many cases, is actually hurting the very people they are supposed to be fighting for.

It is this civil war in the Senate that we all have to start recognizing and deal with. The Senate behavior is disgraceful, and we should, regardless of your party affiliation, as a united American people, finally say "Enough is enough." We need to start getting new Republicans in there and new Democrats in there and Independents in there and people who are actually going to work for the people and not their self-interest or their party interest. If we elect someone to represent us, we should know what they believe and *why* they believe it, but, more importantly, *they* need to know what they believe and why they believe it so that when the time comes, they are willing to break ranks and vote as individuals who represent a larger group of individuals. The behavior in the Senate, well, it is disgraceful.

Father Figure Richard Pryor

"I believe the ability to think is blessed. If you can think about a situation, you can deal with it. The big struggle is to keep your head clear enough to think."

—RICHARD PRYOR

Being independent and having the task of raising myself, to an extent, I also had to figure things out on my own in lieu of benefiting from parental guidance from a father or a strong-minded parental figure. Having no extended family of any kind really involved with my upbringing or education in any active—or even remote—way, I was able to develop my own views, beliefs, perspective, and method of seeing things. I would cherry-pick ideas and ideals from various television role models and athletes and, maybe most importantly, from my favorite forbidden videotape, *Richard Pryor: Live on The Sunset Strip*. Probably the most influential adult male in my life was Richard's stand-up character. Now, I never met Mr. JoJo Walker, but his words were my reality. This obviously is not the parenting tool of choice, and my mother was entirely unaware of my ritual replay of my make-believe father.

Great stories teach you how to tell them. Richard Pryor looked at life in a way that made sense to me and was instructive, especially the message about life experience being vital because you must experience it and survive it to learn from it. When it's ugly, make fun of it. The dark things in life are an undeniable fact of life, but they can't haunt you if you don't carry them with you, and even when they try, you are laughing in their faces as they try to scare you.

Richard made you laugh, and you had to—because if you saw inside him you would cry. This is the same with me and how I treated the things I went through. While at school, I made jokes about whatever situation I was in, and at home, I would be sure to make my mom laugh, even when we were down to only a jar of peanut butter. One of the of the biggest lessons I learned from Richard Pryor was "What makes you laugh can also make you cry." I chose to laugh.

The other pivotal lesson I learned from Richard Pryor was not to fuck with drugs, because he did and it hurt him. Drugs fucked him up and took years off his life. Even worse than that, they made him vulnerable to leeches and gold diggers. Being weak and helpless was something I feared the most at a young age, and seeing his vulnerability and weakness taught me by way of example. Even as a child, I thought being weak was for victims and I was determined that I was never going to be weak; in my eyes, neither was the Richard I admired. It was his drug addiction that burned him. He couldn't quit it. I saw that and decided I was not going to let that happen to me...but we all have our demons and, in my case, they are food, hate, pride, and women.

My point is, we all have demons. Seeing other people's demons come to light makes it so easy to judge because it's not *your* demons and it's not *your* shit—it is *their* shit. The reality is, your shit is just as bad, but the content is different. It becomes easier to judge with moral superiority when your demons are different enough that you can remove yourself from the equation. For example, a professional ball player cheats on his wife and is caught with a hooker and cocaine. His issues are drugs and women and being famous. Yet, every so-called expert weighs in with judgment and this mentality that, "Oh, if that was me, I'd never screw up like that...what a loser, fuckup..." We all have seen that narrative. Well, let's all take a look at the self-proclaimed expert casting judgment and spewing all the self-righteous bullshit about the ball player; that person has their own demons. Maybe he drinks himself to sleep every night and hasn't seen his children in years. The demons are the same, the content is different, and it's easier for talking heads to pretend their demons don't exist by judging others. Maybe if they had Richard as guidance, they would laugh at demons instead.

We all have dirt, lies, skeletons, crimes. Not one individual is clean. I grew up and out of a closet full of skeletons brimming with corpses of my own lies and secrets; those skeletons forced me to learn that everybody has something to hide, and those skeletons will never let me forget that. Yeah, my upbringing was rough, sure, but the kid two houses down from me had to fight his stepdad off him every night. I'm sure he would've gladly come home to a note instead. Someone always has it worse, and your own situation can always get worse—and it will if you let it. That is my thought process.

My world view and perspective were heavily shaped by growing up in "the dark." The dark molded me. I excelled in the dark, that place where most people allow themselves to be swallowed during a bad period in their life. Some people make excuses for tough, dark times in their lives. Not me; I don't lay any excuses on my dark times. I know that when I screw up, it's because I'm screwing up. This is the note I write to myself: "Own it." Looking at things from the inside out means judging myself as I would judge others. And that works for me.

It is also worth noting that I grew up without religion to influence or train my thought process. I was drawn to dinosaurs because there was proof of their existence—they left "'notes" in the form of fossils. Not to mention, the few run-ins I had with "men of god" were...well, less than stellar, and usually those folks turned out to be some of the creepiest, most racist individuals I ever met. Religion just wasn't anything I wanted to be a part of. I don't have issues with someone being religious because I judge from inside out. I believe what I believe based on my life experience, and I always assume that other people do as well. However, I do struggle with a lot of religious people who believe what they do just because that's what they have been told and who think they are all-knowing because of what they've been told to believe. They're sheep, for lack of a better term, and I can't stand them.

Kinda Black

Learning about race at a young age really changed the way I looked at race. Being painfully aware of this at a young age is more than just growing up, but it isn't a bad thing. For me, it is a power you can take away from those who want to use your race against you. I'm Black. I don't believe in biracial anything. In our history of the United States, the only history I know and frankly care about, you can be anything you want, and you don't have to be anything you don't want. There is no such thing as "half white" in our society. Now, I admit I do not know if this is negative, positive, or just a straight mean, but let me explain.

I have been in a room with the nicest white people on the planet—decent, charity-giving, kindhearted people—but the first thing they would say to me, with no ill intent, was "Are you Black?" Noticing the difference. Wanting to see and define exactly what I am. Now you take that same room and replace those white people with two average, African-American Black Brothers, they will look in the room, then look at me and smile and say, "You *Black*." Less of a question. More of a cultural connection. White people *see* the difference—Black people *embrace* the difference.

I was raised by a white mother who did everything she could to avoid addressing the difference within the circumstances she was dealt, that is, being with a black man and raising mixed-race kids. Without my Black father around, who neither had the time, the energy, nor the skillset to be a "dad," I was in a position where I was forced to learn my way through life the hard way because my mother was not equipped to deal with the circumstances other than "your mother loves you and wants to protect you and keep you safe." The two things my biological father gave me were DNA—the genetics of ruthless aggression—and a shining example of the person I raised myself *not* to be.

I really learned the most about racism and what it means to be different from the people within the branches of my family tree. My grandfather made it clear to me when I was four years old. My grandfather was a proud man. A hard-working man. He was loved by his family and community. He was a man who rescued his young daughter from a bad situation that life had dealt her, one riddled with domestic violence and poverty. When that man, my grandfather, met his grandsons, he looked us over good, evaluating my hands and face before stating, "He can't live here, he's got too much nigger in him...same with the other one." Was this evil or honest? Two things can be true at once. All that mattered was that, at that moment, I knew I was different, and I also realized I was going to be separated from my mother. My mother and I had been through so many battles together I thought the only thing that would separate us was death, but in this case, it was my skin color. I always respected my grandfather's hard work, his "tell it like it is even when it's wrong" attitude, because his hard truth forced me to look at things for what they *are*, not what they *should* be... and to never sugarcoat shit. Would it have been better if he agreed to keep me, inevitably ignore me, slap me around, hide me from his world, and openly resent my existence? These are the obvious "what ifs," but that is not what happened. It happened just how I just said it did.

Near the end of my grandfather's life, I visited him. It was clear we didn't have much use for each other by that time. Despite this, we could still watch a John Wayne movie or *The Three Stooges*. My grandfather never lied to me, always maintained his painful honesty that caused me to resent him. I always wanted to prove him wrong. At the very end, knowing he was dying, he said, "George, I was wrong about you. You ended up a strong, good man." I responded with "You're going to ruin the movie, old man." He laughed. A few days later, he passed away. This is not a redemption tale. A man on his deathbed saying a kind word in his final hours of life was not the man he was...and I know that. Whatever his motives, up until that point, I knew the man he was, and, if nothing else, that is what I respected about him—racist or not—his brutal and at times humiliating and painful honesty. I never loved my grandfather, nor did I fear him, but I always wanted to be better than his stereotype and bigotry. At the same time, I respected him immensely for always keeping it real. His honesty left no room for a grey area, so I always knew where I stood. You can coexist with people when you understand what they stand for.

Here is another example of how no one is clean—on either side: a college girlfriend of mine noticed that I never traveled "home" or saw my family over breaks or holidays and wanted to surprise me with a gesture to help me "connect" with family she knew I hadn't seen since she met me. Although the intent was pure and meant to be a positive experience for me, she did not know my family history, and there was a mix-up concerning my last name.

As I said in an earlier chapter, I left home at age sixteen. I left following a fight with my stepfather that left him with a broken eye socket, slightly fractured jaw, and a concussion. I packed a trash bag with what I had and left my home and him behind me. As a result, that is largely why, while attending college, I never traveled home, not for holidays or any breaks. My experiences are my own and I never broadcasted my life story, so those around me didn't know much, if anything, about my home life or family situation—nor did I find it necessary for them to know. Nonetheless, this soon-to-be-ex girlfriend of mine took it upon herself to look up my last name from my birth certificate that I had lying around my dorm room. In doing so, she assumed that my last name of Murdoch was my father's family name. She was wrong; I switched my last name when I started playing sports. I knew seeing that name hurt my mom's feelings and I was the man of our house, so on the first day at my new school, I changed it by telling the office it was a mistake. I convinced them that Clements was not my name and that it was Murdoch. I remember the old lady with the beehive hairdo just shrugged her shoulders and assumed that the intake lady screwed it up. I was Murdoch from that day forward.

Now back to the hypocrisy of racism. That ex-girlfriend planned for me to fly to Massachusetts to meet the Clements family (who she mistakenly reached out to, hoping for some grand family reunion). She thought she was reuniting me with my mom's family, but she was wrong—she'd reached out to good old dad's side. Finally, after a lot of convincing, we ultimately flew out there to meet them.

I remember the house was old; it smelled like wet carpet and dog. This house was built for four, but it was housing fourteen. At least they were a family that supported each other. My grandmother embraced her role of the family matriarch and ruled the domain, which included her fifteen sons and daughters and an army of grandkids, cousins, and more. She was the boss. Seeing her was a powerful moment and feeling of immense disconnect simultaneously. I didn't have any semblance of "family" growing up, but while having dinner with them it was clear they were very poor but proud. Grandmother, whom I had not seen or interacted with since I was about three or four years old, took it upon herself to sit down with me and actually instruct me on what I needed to do to "improve the family name." Grandmother, who I never had any cute nickname for as we hardly knew each other, was mahogany black with cold blue eyes. She said, "George you are a 'strong Black man'...and 'special'...." I asked her if (and obviously hoped that) she was telling me this because there was a pride in my ancestry, like maybe my great-great grandfather was an African king, or Frederick Douglass; you know, something cool. No. She went on to tell me that since I was light-skinned, and, in her words, "they" had "worked very hard to make me light," that I could "get a good job."

She continued to tell me how it was going to be by specifically detailing who I was to procreate with and who I was not to. So, get this, my grandmother's explicit instructions were as follows:

1. I was *not* to have a child with anyone darker than myself. If I did, I would screw everything up that "they" had apparently "worked hard" on. Plus, it was hard being Black, but *worse* to be dark! Yeah, okay...I just nodded along.

2. Grandma then gave me a list of acceptable races to comingle and procreate with. The verbal list of acceptable races was as follows: 1. Asian. They were "good with money" and likely an accountant. 2. White, blonde, blue eyes. They had "money."

3. *No* Jews. They were "scheming" and "out to get you." Hard no.

4. Finally, absolutely *no* Blacks or Latinos...ever.

211

The final thing she said before we rejoined the group was in reference to my "girlfriend" (who was with me), saying, "Good job by the way...the white girl, good job." That girl and I broke up soon after we got back to Nebraska.

I found out that even my Black family hated people, too. That they were full of that type of in-house, racist shit in my family tree with the backwards-ass thinking of, "Yes we are Black, but whitey likes *us* better than the *darker ones*." It felt like I somehow was in a time warp and had slipped into a different timeline where the civil war is between African-Americans.

I know there is white on white racism, too, like the Irish don't like the Scottish or the Australians don't like the New Zealanders and vise-versa, but this was a complete betrayal to me! It was worse than anything my grandfather on my white mother's side ever said to me. He was honest, and I knew where we stood. But this woman, my grandmother... she was transparent to me. It was clear that she hated herself, her people, and thought it an accomplishment to spread that hate by encouraging procreation that falls within her realm of acceptable racial partners. Although I nodded along politely, I nonetheless instantly realized I wanted nothing to do with her.

I was born hardwired to view my difference not as just being "other" but rather as powerful, like a superhero who cannot be objectified. There is specific genre of rough experiences for my light skin. Being light-skinned, I was on the receiving end of the negatives without the positives. Given that, having a great right hook came in handy. Black people had the mentality "you aren't Black enough" and white folks had the mentality of "you don't belong here." You got special privileges for not being Black enough, but there was also a fear of "if my child mixes with you...."

All my bumps and scars are because of this. Not of being a victim, but lessons from my reality. It gave me the ability to accept anyone the way they were because I didn't identify with a particular group, never grew roots, and kept things short, sweet, fun, and tribal.

I am or have been a blue-chip, all-American, talented college athlete; a college graduate; a liar, cheater, manipulator; an animal enthusiast; a smart-ass (a personal point of pride); a rude bully; a lost, angry bar cook. I've been fucked over, hated on, fired, passed over, judged; a target of attempted lynching (but it didn't work out for them); a police brutality survivor; "that nigger," "a nigger," "my nigger." I've had a gun to my head twice; had my heart broken; had it put it back together again...but I've never been a victim.

Acknowledgments

I would like to acknowledge the following individuals that helped me along the way to get where I am today.

My mother could have had an abortion and no one would have questioned her at fifteen years old. But she chose to have me.

The Isles for giving me a work ethic.

Coach de Shane kicked me off the team and made me grow up.

Mr. Ray made education fun.

Coach Martinez, you saved my life.

Coach Morris challenged me to be better.

Coach Hoffman made me love the weight room.

Dr. Bishop for wisdom.

Dr. Lacey for understanding what it is to be a Black man.

Ve Sean, SNU.

Rico, Blaze of Glory.

Big Corn family, for advice on being a real man.

Big Tob, friend for life.

Tiny, you know!

Keys, do the job.

Snoop, keeping it real and then doing the work.

Larry Pollock, smartest business man I've ever met and no bullshit ever.

Kevin Barkey, cart wheels and be careful.

The American Dream, Dusty Rhodes for teaching me about painting my canvases. I was proud to be "yours and pay for your sins."

Triple H and Stephanie; true professionals.

PJ Black, true friend and brother in life.

Kevin Kylie, "In Marinvich we trust."

Ec3, whelp Cleveland.

Dolph, don't let me suplex you, brother!

Santino, TJ Tivita, JTG, Eric Sunny, Afa Jr. Trinity, Uso's swagger, MVP Chavo Guerrero, Drew McIntrye, Bobby Lashley, Chris "Boar" Bell, Randy Orton, Chris Masters, Trevor Murdoch, The Major Brothers, Luke Gallows, James Storm, Kurt Angle, Mark Henry, B.I.G. Show, Jinder Mahal, Scott Armstrong, Bones and Spider, Titus O'Neal, Edge, Christian Matt Hardy, Alberto Del Rio, Lord Steven Regal, Cesaro, Cody Rhodes, Dustin "Chicken" Rhodes, Fred Young (sorry about the elbow),

University of Kansas at Kearney offensive line; Chad Vokune, Todd Peters, Sean Evans, Cory Williams, Diesel, Martin Simmons.

Antelope Valley Jr. College offensive line; Randy Clemens will knight, Brian Lasagna, Sean Evans, Mr. and Mrs. Evans.

Tommy Dreamer for seeing something I didn't in me.

Arn Anderson, great coach, all those sweaty shirts.

John Laurinaitis, thank you two times for WWE and giving me the opportunity of a lifetime.

Bill DeMott, coach of the highest order.

King Biscuit, thank you for pushing me and making me prove I wanted it!

Acknowledgments

Dr. Tom Pritchard, in the big picture, brilliant coach and teacher.

Jody Hamilton, "Flatter than piss on a platter," always the assassin.

Steve Keirn, earning your respect and working at FCW, thank you.

Dr. Death, Steve Williams, Animal! Tough coaches, proud to be one of your guys!

Ricky Steamboat, "gear changes!" Thank you, coach, and thank you for WrestleMania 3.

Dean Malenko, I got my boots!

Road Dog, thank you great agent and teacher and we gotta do it in Memphis Texas will shit on it! No we doing it in Texas has to be Texas!

Heath Slater, I'm the lawn mower!

Santino and Idle, lifelong friends!

Tensai, the tag partner I always wanted, not sure you were that thrilled but thank you for tons of funk and your awesome parents! A real pro!

Mark Corrano, a lot of people down on you! Thank you.

Joseph Way, we made chicken salad.

Phil, stiff drink please, and Martell!!!!

Vince McMahon, the boss period.

Kevin Dunn, nice fuckin braces!

Michael Cole, bar Tuesdays!

JR Jim Ross, you gave my dream in the ring a voice and no one does it better.

Gorilla Monsoon, a father.

King Haku, hero in life, my hero.

Mike Bucci, thanks for the chairs and the raise.

Kevin Nash, broken beer bottles.

John Cena, thank you for opening Hard Nocks South and thank you for my WrestleMania moment.

Mark Henry, mentor and friend.

Kane, great role model.

Daniel Bryant, great dad story's.

Big E, worst godfather ever, I say that with love!

Kofi, Boston proud!

T.J. Wilson, thank you for Mexico and great friendship.

Kurt Angle, you are the definition of redemption and that's a fact.

KMac, great coach, enjoyed going at it on the practice field.

Greg Gutfeld, thank you for having the courage to break the mold and giving a brother a shot! The find!

Kat, co-captain!

Juan Williams, always making me welcome great advice.

Dana Perino, greatest mentor ever.

Jasper, RIP.

Mike Rotunda, best agent ever!

Megan Albano, THANK YOU!

Jason Devon for more podcasts like this!

Chris Epting, for writing this book with me and the very definition of class act and friendship.

Walter Kern, life changing perspective and friend.

Rob Long, genius.

Billy Corgan, thanks for the redemption.

Suzanne Scott, thank you, Boss!

Tom, hellava ride so far.

Holly, get back to work.

Jacob and Anthony and everyone else at Post Hill Press, Thank you!

Acknowledgments

To Tayna, my lawyer, you are as cool as you are ruthless in fighting for what's right! And sticking by me when things got rough.

To my agent, Maura, thanks for taking a chance on me!

Joan, thank you.

Special thanks to Lou Ferrigno. As the character "Hulk" you gave me courage as a child. I wanted to be strong like you, fair like you, powerful and that inspired me my whole life. Meeting you on my show and talking with you and your incredible family reaffirmed that I picked the right hero. Thank you, sir!

Rob, Hard Nock South, thank you for allowing me to win my life back, train in the gym and be a part of a brotherhood. We did more than lift, we walked through fires together, became a family, and the stories I could tell, but if you're not in Hard Nocks South it's none of your fuckin' business! But we are all glorious unicorns of FUCK! Thank you, Rob!

If I left anyone out, my bad.

Oh, and last but not least, Dad, thank you for never being there. Thank you for never showing me your ideals of manhood or a hard days' work or how to treat women or your own children. Thank you for not being there. Because if you were there I'd be just like you...so good looking out. I learned from other men. I embraced accomplishments and accountability and I'm better in life than you ever could understand. It took a village, it took some failures and broken hearts and mid-meal cramps, it took doubt, it took anger and it took forgiving myself and ultimately forgiving you. I hated you most of my life for not trying. Now I understand some people get knocked down and answer the count and some just lay there. You couldn't get up and lucky for me it's not genetic thing, it's a you thing...thanks #nuffsaid.

About the Author

A 6′8″, 350-pound behemoth Tyrus is an affable, hard-working entertainer with a sly sense of humor. Following his initial calling to football, he became a bouncer at numerous establishments in Los Angeles where he caught the attention of Snoop Dogg and became his bodyguard. That drew the attention of the WWE where he went on to enjoy success as "Brodus Clay" and, later, "The Funkasaurus," which led to his starring in Mattel commercials and appearing in WWE video games. Along with working as an actor in film and television, he is a frequent featured guest on Fox News and *The Greg Gutfeld Show*.